The Anglo-Saxons

An Enthralling Overview of the People and History of England from the Early Middle Ages to the Battle of Hastings

© Copyright 2024 - All rights reserved.

The content contained within this book may not be reproduced, duplicated, or transmitted without direct written permission from the author or the publisher.

Under no circumstances will any blame or legal responsibility be held against the publisher, or author, for any damages, reparation, or monetary loss due to the information contained within this book, either directly or indirectly.

Legal Notice:

This book is copyright protected. It is only for personal use. You cannot amend, distribute, sell, use, quote, or paraphrase any part, or the content within this book, without the consent of the author or publisher.

Disclaimer Notice:

Please note the information contained within this document is for educational and entertainment purposes only. All effort has been executed to present accurate, up-to-date, reliable, and complete information. No warranties of any kind are declared or implied. Readers acknowledge that the author is not engaging in the rendering of legal, financial, medical, or professional advice. The content within this book has been derived from various sources. Please consult a licensed professional before attempting any techniques outlined in this book.

By reading this document, the reader agrees that under no circumstances is the author responsible for any losses, direct or indirect, that are incurred as a result of the use of the information contained within this document, including, but not limited to, errors, omissions, or inaccuracies.

Free limited time bonus

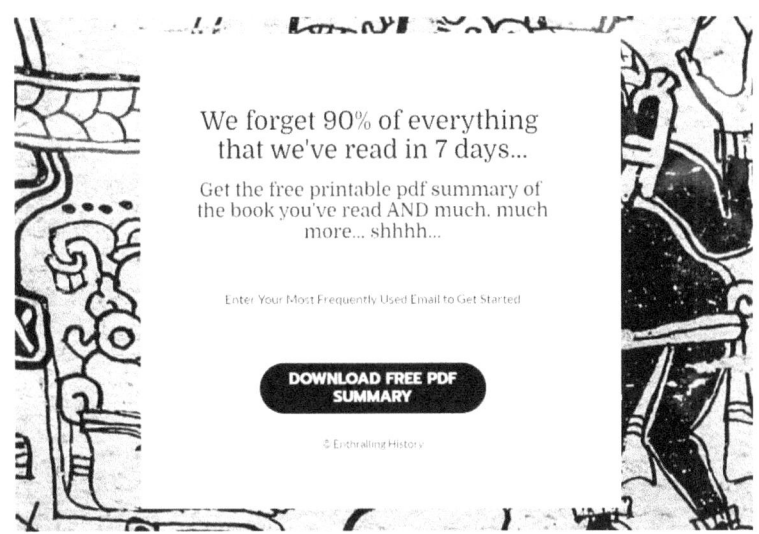

Stop for a moment. We have a free bonus set up for you. The problem is this: we forget 90% of everything that we read after 7 days. Crazy fact, right? Here's the solution: we've created a printable, 1-page pdf summary for this book that you're reading now. All you have to do to get your free pdf summary is to go to the following website: https://livetolearn.lpages.co/enthrallinghistory/

Or, Scan the QR code!

Once you do, it will be intuitive. Enjoy, and thank you!

Table of Contents

INTRODUCTION 1
CHAPTER ONE – THE END OF ROMAN RULE IN BRITAIN 4
CHAPTER TWO – THE ARRIVAL OF THE ANGLO-SAXONS IN BRITAIN 18
CHAPTER THREE – THE BIRTH OF ANGLO-SAXON ENGLAND 28
CHAPTER FOUR – MERCIAN SUPREMACY..46
CHAPTER FIVE – ANGLO-SAXONS AND THE VIKING AGE 63
CHAPTER SIX – THE MAKING OF ENGLAND..88
CHAPTER SEVEN – FROM ÆTHELRED THE UNREADY TO WILLIAM THE CONQUEROR 102
CONCLUSION 121
HERE'S ANOTHER BOOK BY ENTHRALLING HISTORY THAT YOU MIGHT LIKE..125
FREE LIMITED TIME BONUS...126
SOURCES 127

Introduction

Hearing the name "Anglo-Saxon" produces many different sentiments in both casual and curious students of history. Indeed, even though this name is recognizable to most, there have been many changing perceptions and even myths regarding this group of people.

We have a general idea of who the Anglo-Saxons were and where they lived. Most people are aware that the term describes an ethnocultural group that dwelled in the British Isles during the Middle Ages. In fact, until developments in recent scholarship (made possible in part by new archeological discoveries), the generally held belief was that the Anglo-Saxons occupied a place between Rome and William the Conqueror in Britain's history. This concept came from the far more widespread popularity of these two historical benchmarks, but it should not reduce the importance of the Anglo-Saxons in English and European history.

But why exactly? In what ways are the Anglo-Saxons relevant today? Behind the veil of mystery that surrounds the Anglo-Saxons lies the dynamic culture of a unique people. So profoundly did this culture exert its influence during the Early Middle Ages that its legacies can be observed at first glance. To begin with, the group of people we refer to as Anglo-Saxons are responsible for the language this book is written in. Modern English directly descends from the language these people spoke—Old English. They also gave England its name—the land of the Angles—and established the first English kingdoms from which a unified Kingdom of England would arise in the tenth century.

The Anglo-Saxons, once pagan Germanic invaders, were responsible for sowing the social and cultural seeds that shaped England, including conversion to Christianity. Some of the most recognizable and oldest centers of English Christian practices, including Canterbury, York, Rochester, and Winchester, all date back to the age of the Anglo-Saxons. Even the current English administration system can be traced back to the Anglo-Saxons, who reshaped and revived the settlement patterns of post-Roman Britain after the old Roman centers were decimated.

All this, combined with an amazing cultural and material heritage and a compelling history, certainly makes it clear that the Anglo-Saxons are very much relevant.

Still, before we dive deep into the history of the Anglo-Saxons, we must consider an important detail: to whom exactly does this term refer? Problems arise when assigning ethnonyms to groups of people from the past, especially considering that the Early Middle Ages, also referred to as the Dark Ages, are notorious for failing to produce many written records. We will analyze the emergence of the term "Anglo-Saxon" in more detail in the chapters that follow, but we must establish here that the Anglo-Saxons are an identifiable and distinct group that can be adequately studied.

The people whose history we are about to recount did not necessarily refer to themselves as Anglo-Saxons. However, sources first began to use this distinction in the eighth century. King Alfred the Great, one of the most prominent figures from the period, referred to himself as "King of the Anglo-Saxons" in the second half of the ninth century. As we will come to see, the name "Anglo-Saxon" has been used at times to combine many important attributes into one cultural, religious, linguistic, national, social, or ethnic identity. We will explore exactly how these identities were utilized in varying contexts.

This book thus focuses on telling the history of the Anglo-Saxons, the distinct group of people that dominated post-Roman England in the Early Middle Ages until their eventual defeat by William the Conqueror in 1066. In the opening chapters, we will look at Britain under late Roman control, discussing the socio-political and cultural impact the Romans left on the island as they were gradually ousted by migratory barbarians. Then, we will look at the collapse of Roman rule in Britain and the gradual replacement of Roman society by the Anglo-Saxons.

The middle chapters of the book will be concerned with the establishment of Anglo-Saxon society in Britain, including the era of Christianization that was ushered in from the seventh century onward. Christianization came hand-in-hand with the emergence of the first political entities in England, which we can call kingdoms. Over the years, territorial and political differences between these kingdoms increased until the old tribal chiefdoms were replaced by a method of political organization greatly influenced by Christianity.

We will also examine the cultural and socio-economic developments that gave rise to this unique civilization in the British Isles. We will explore the history of the early Anglo-Saxon kingdoms that battled among themselves for dominance before they came across their most dangerous enemy yet—the Vikings. The complex relationships that would emerge between the Anglo-Saxons and the Vikings would shape the final part of the Anglo-Saxon's history.

The final chapters of the book will cover the Norman Conquest of England and its aftermath. In addition to immediate political consequences, this included the acceptance, gradual modification, and appropriation of the Anglo-Saxon history of England.

Chapter One – The End of Roman Rule in Britain

In this chapter, we will briefly summarize the history of Roman rule in Britain and discuss the final years of Britannia as a Roman province. After taking hold of Britannia in the late first century AD, the Romans lost control at the beginning of the fifth century AD. Even though Britain lay at the edge of the Roman Empire, it was well integrated by the fourth century AD. The free local Briton population of the island, who were of Celtic origin, were full-fledged citizens of Rome by the time the empire started to experience prolonged periods of domestic and external crises. This chapter will thus examine the nature of Roman control over Britain and the gradual decline of Roman rule on the island.

Roman Britain

Britain, or Britannia as it was called by the Romans, was one of the most unique provinces of the Roman Empire. The first Roman expeditions to Britain were famously organized by Julius Caesar when he crossed the English Channel twice during his conquests of Gaul. These expeditions in 55 and 54 BC achieved little territorial gain. The conquest of Britain did not properly begin until 43 AD under Emperor Claudius.

Even before Caesar, however, the local Briton population of the island was under the Roman sphere of influence, trading heavily with merchants from neighboring Roman provinces. By 77 AD, Wales was conquered. For the rest of the century, Roman legions under General Gnaeus Julius Agricola continued to assert Roman power in the northern part of the island. Eventually, in 122 AD, the northern border of the province was established with the construction of Hadrian's Wall—a defensive structure that stretched the length of the island along the River Tyne. Built to deter invasions from the ever-so-zealous northern Celtic tribes, it marked the extent of direct Roman control over Britain and continued to play its part very well for the next two centuries.

Britannia was one of the farthest-lying provinces of the vast Roman Empire that, at its peak, exerted its influence as far as Mesopotamia. The fact that it was a large island outside of *Mare Nostrum*—"Our Sea" as the Mediterranean was referred to by the Romans—made its control even more remarkable. In terms of utility, Britain was nothing special for Rome, at least in economic terms. It had a terrible climate and was characterized by a lack of arable land in its western and northern parts, which made the practice of large-scale agriculture very difficult. Some of the island's products, such as tin, were highly valuable, but this was not nearly enough to propel Britannia to the status of a profitable Roman province, especially considering the riches with which other distant lands supplied Rome.

Considering Britannia's relative economic unimportance, it might seem strange that it housed a significant portion of the Roman legions as early as the mid-second century. Up to 50,000 Roman soldiers were stationed on the island, a number that constituted about a tenth of the Roman army. These soldiers mainly guarded the western and northernmost frontiers of Britannia, supported by a network of forts.

Nevertheless, the process of Britain's Romanization was slow and gradual. Eventually, Rome achieved its goals there as well as it had elsewhere, primarily because the benefits the Romans brought were immense. The main benefits for the local people were security and interconnectedness with the rest of the "civilized" world, which meant economic and sociocultural integration. Britain became a normal Roman province, and its population rightfully considered themselves Roman.

The Romans' extensive military presence on the island no doubt accelerated their control of Britannia and rendered possible resistance from the locals useless. In fact, there is no record of a large-scale, united revolt against Roman rule in Britain until well into the fourth century. By this time, the Roman Empire was steadily in decline. In just two hundred years, the Romans radically transformed the everyday life of Britannia, and the province seemed to accept its new role as part of the cosmopolitan Roman world.

In 197, fifty years after the establishment of Hadrian's Wall as the province's northern border, Britannia was divided into two administrative units—Upper and Lower Britannia. Then, a hundred years later, under Emperor Diocletian, new administrative divisions were implemented. By 314, the Roman province was made up of four such units. The north, with its capital at York, was reorganized into Britannia Secunda; the west, including the Roman possessions in Wales, was named Britannia Prima, with Cirencester likely its capital; the central-eastern part of the island became Flavia Caesariensis, centered around Lincoln; and, finally, the southern part of Britain was called Maxima Caesariensis, which housed London and was the most socio-economically advanced of the four.

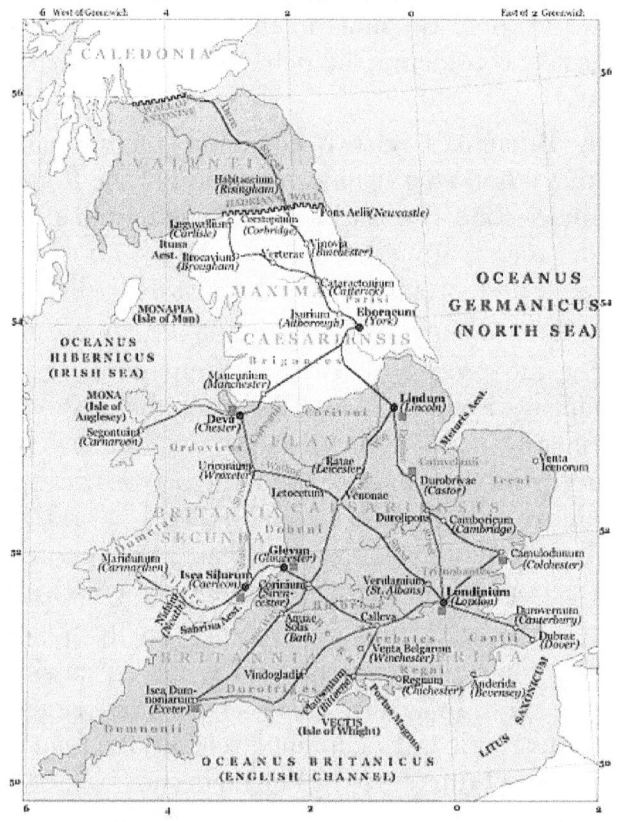

Map of Roman Britain.
https://commons.wikimedia.org/wiki/File:Roman_Britain_410.jpg

The Romans made London the administrative center of the province, building on the importance of the town before their arrival. Here dwelt the *vicarius,* the emperor's representative and the most important Roman administrator on the island. The *vicarius* was responsible for governing the province and reported directly to the emperor. Governors of the four sub-provinces of Britannia, on the other hand, were more involved in day-to-day bureaucracy—the collection of taxes, settling of legal disputes, maintaining public order, and employment of civil servants.

Records indicate that the individuals holding these offices were directly appointed by the central Roman government and were frequently changed to avoid the abuse of power. This was, nevertheless, frequent. Roman bureaucracy was full of power-hungry individuals, and corruption was rampant in Britain, just like in any other Roman province. It was, in fact, far easier to practice corruption in Britain considering there was no efficient way for the emperors to impose their authority on such a remote province. They relied heavily on the goodwill of their appointed governors.

The Romanization of Britain's settlements can be observed both in descriptions of them in primary sources and archeological evidence. After the Roman conquest, different tribes led by their respective chieftains at first continued to dominate and organize in broadly defined areas. These domains of the old tribal chiefdoms were called civitates, and the towns and settlements that fell under their rough borders soon bore the marks of Roman influence.

The relative peace and security the Romans brought indirectly resulted in the continual growth of Britannia's population. This growth accelerated the process of urbanization. The biggest towns were soon organized in a way that was profoundly Roman, with gridded streets and a city center that contained a forum market, public baths, and administrative buildings. The larger towns regularly hosted traders and farmers from the countryside, who came to these centers to pursue business. The Romans also devoted great attention to building walls around the cities, an important feature of Celtic towns even before the arrival of the Romans. Most stone walls were constructed under the supervision of Roman armies in the third century.

The civitates were governed by local councils that worked hand-in-hand with appointed Roman officials to maintain public order and regulate public life. Only certain men were eligible to become members of these councils, referred to as decurions, and the bureaucrats would often reward them for their dedication and distinguishments with promotions.

The countryside of Britain also came to resemble the typical Roman countryside seen in provinces that had been under Roman control for many centuries, such as Italy or Iberia. The decurions usually came from wealthier families that owned land outside of the towns. Archeological evidence has revealed that they most likely lived in estates that greatly resembled Italian villas in all aspects, most importantly in their grandeur or lavishness. Some of these villas, constructed in the third and fourth centuries, were made from imported materials and feature characteristics such as mosaic floors with depictions of Roman mythology. The villas were surrounded by farmland and smaller dwellings, most likely designated to free peasants or slaves who worked for the estates' wealthy owners. Of course, the countryside from the times of Roman Britain also housed small villages and farmsteads, where the lower classes of society lived.

The economy of Roman Britain, as we mentioned earlier, was nothing special. Much like everywhere else, it was heavily tied to urban or rural life and sometimes even regulated with legislation. For example, British towns were full of different craftsmen, such as tailors, carpenters, smiths, and weavers, who had to pass down their professions to their children as part of Roman law. Doctors, lawyers, and teachers, though less numerous, also made up the cities' workforce. Pottery was one of the most important products, not only in domestic markets but also in other Roman provinces.

Finally, the cultural makeup of Roman Britannia was very interesting. Just like in other provinces of the empire, the Roman imperial cult, which venerated the emperors and Rome itself, was integrated into the local religious beliefs of the Britons. Rome had a relatively tolerant relationship with local traditions and belief systems as long as the newly integrated populations respected Roman customs and recognized the superiority of Roman culture. In Britain, for example, the Roman pantheon of gods and the cult of Augustus, the emperor after whom the imperial cult became especially prominent, were venerated. Temples were constructed in Britain's cities, and evidence shows that the population actively followed ritual practices. Over time, the gods in the equally diverse Celtic pantheon were associated with their Roman counterparts. This, combined with the imposition of otherwise all-encompassing Roman civilization, meant that Britons were well-assimilated Roman citizens.

Profound cultural changes would start to take place in Britain in the fourth century as the Roman Empire began to tolerate and eventually accept Christianity as its official religion. For the first few centuries since the advent of Christianity in Roman Judaea, Roman emperors had exercised different rates of tolerance.

The reasons for the initial widespread dislike of Christianity were multifold. First, there was the odd nature of the belief system and its rituals. A more important factor, caused by the relatively rapid and multi-regional growth of the religion, was that it undermined Roman religious, cultural, and political authority. The persecution of Christianity reached its peak with the reign of Diocletian, who, alongside his co-rulers, issued a series of edicts in the early fourth century that severely restricted Christian worship and rights.

In Britain, the most prominent example of persecution was Saint Alban—who is considered the first recorded British Christian martyr. Under Emperor Constantine the Great, however, persecution of Christianity would stop after about 312. According to the legend, Constantine came to believe in the Christian God after witnessing a vision of the cross before an important and difficult battle. After achieving victory, Constantine began discouraging the persecution of Christians and actively promoted the religion, giving Christian clergy the right to peaceful assembly and practice. Thus, we know that three bishops from Britain were present at the Synod of Arles, held in Roman Gaul in 314.

Threats to Roman Britain

By the late third century, Roman Britain essentially included territories in most of modern-day England and the easternmost parts of Wales. Though several Roman generals campaigned in the Scottish Highlands soon after arriving in Britain, the Romans had abandoned their efforts to conquer the northernmost areas of the island (modern-day Scotland), as we mentioned earlier. The forts along Hadrian's Wall were manned at all times. However, this is not to say there was no contact with the Celtic tribes that lived north of the wall. Archeological evidence suggests that the tribes were dependent on the Romans for trade. Excavated settlement sites north of Hadrian's Wall bear many similarities with those in the territories under direct Roman control.

In Wales, the Roman influence was not as long-lasting despite the Romans' extensive campaigns there during the first century. This was partially because of the mountainous terrain of Wales and the lack of good infrastructure, which meant the region was not as interconnected with the rest of Britain. The military garrisons initially stationed in the most western Roman forts in Wales seem to have been abandoned by the fourth century, and there are considerably fewer Roman-style villas in Wales than in England.

Roman control was threatened by barbarians who lived outside of these rough borders. The most well-known enemies of the Romans in Britain were the Picts ("the painted ones"), who dwelled in the Scottish Highlands. The Picts would usually launch their attacks on the richer eastern ports of Roman Britannia.

The Picts are considered the descendants of the older Caledonii people, who lived in northern Britain before the arrival of the Romans. Much as with other tribes, we know very little about the Picts despite the compelling cultural heritage they left, including large stones that contain complex ornamental carvings. These Pictish carved stones were probably used for border demarcations and gravestones and are mostly found in east and central Scotland, dating to about the seventh century.

Roman shores were also subject to raids from Irish Celts, especially from the Scotti, one of the most widely mentioned barbarian tribes in ancient sources. Their culture is somewhat different from that of the other Celtic peoples of Britain, which can be logically attributed to the geographic separation of the islands.

Interestingly, the most feared barbarians that posed a threat to Britain during Roman rule were the seafaring tribes from northern Germany and the Danish peninsula, namely the Saxons, Angles, and Jutes. The Romans identified them all simply as Saxons, a term that would be later used to distinguish between the eventual Anglo-Saxon inhabitants of Britain and the Saxons who lived in continental Europe. After the second century, frequent contact between the Saxons and the Romans resulted in these barbarian societies' advancements in metallurgy, with the use of gold, silver, and bronze in weapons as well as for decorative purposes.

Of course, Britain was not the only province in the Roman Empire that suffered from regular barbarian invasions. This was the case everywhere in the European provinces. The containment of these invasions, most of which were relatively small-scale, was possible if a constant military presence was maintained at the border. This presence depended on multiple things. Firstly, it depended on the treatment of soldiers and the existing infrastructure—if and how soldiers were paid, their living conditions, the maintenance of roads and communications, and the steadiness of supplies to the frontier positions. Secondly, the defense of Rome's borders against the barbarians also depended on those in charge. Rome's history can be analyzed by observing the reigns of different emperors because they made decisions regarding every aspect of Roman life—above all, military affairs.

It was, of course, the unlimited authority of emperors that allowed them to exert such a direct influence on their domains. However, problems would often arise before the next designated emperor obtained the power and authority necessary to be recognized as emperor. In the Roman Empire, the transfer of power from one emperor to the next was notoriously complicated. The practice of the emperors choosing their successors rarely worked, and the vastness of the empire permitted many usurpers to challenge their authority.

In most cases, the usurpers were military leaders who had gained loyalty and support from their troops and had led their forces in the most distant parts of the Roman Empire. Each general was in command of tens of thousands of troops—a number necessary to maintain control in the many provinces of Rome. These generals often promised their soldiers glory and riches in exchange for their support in the fight for the title of emperor. The soldiers, out of loyalty forged after years of command, championed their leaders. Often, there were multiple "usurper emperors" at once, all claiming their authority in different provinces of the empire. This meant that the actual emperor, who had nominally inherited the title from his predecessor, had to defeat them in battle to properly be *the* Emperor of Rome.

In Britain, however, until the late third century, there were fewer problems with poor military maintenance and potential usurpers. This meant that, despite being a frontier province of the Roman Empire, Britain held its own against barbarian incursions. Troops were constantly stationed on the frontiers and enjoyed good conditions in the forts they occupied. The most important British towns were also walled by the third century, different from similar old towns in Gaul, which only began to build significant stone defenses after the reign of Emperor Aurelian

(270-275).

The Roman emperors during the second half of the third century, Aurelian, Probus, and Diocletian, were all veteran generals who had gained experience fighting in the east against far more technologically advanced powers. After gaining power, they bolstered the defenses in the most vulnerable Roman provinces.

In Britain, this also meant reinforcing the system of forts and devoting more resources to the Roman garrisons. As the Saxon incursions on the eastern shores of England intensified by the late third century, the Roman authorities upgraded the defensive capabilities of coastal towns and harbors and established new forts between major cities. These measures aimed to not only dissuade barbarians from trying to attack the shores of Britain but also keep the rogue barbarian bands from reaching the heart of the island.

A Roman military commander of Belgian origin, Marcus Carausius, had been made commander of the Roman navy in the English Channel thanks to his proficiency at fighting barbarians. The navy was to defend the shores of northern Gaul and Britannia from the raids of the Saxon and Frank barbarians. Carausius' position was a very powerful one, entrusting him command over thousands of men. In 286, however, Roman Augustus Maximian blamed Carausius for collaborating with the barbarians and abusing his powers. There is no evidence that Maximian's charges against Carausius were justified, but Carausius, in response, declared himself the emperor of Britain and Gaul and openly rebelled against the central imperial authority. Carausius held considerably more sway than Maximian may have had, derived from the fact that Maximian's attack on Carausius' position in 289 was repelled.

Carausius stayed in power in northern Gaul and Britain. He bolstered his defenses and even minted his own coins, paying the imperial soldiers stationed in the territories he controlled. Historians believe this might suggest that he viewed himself as an equal to the Roman Caesars and enjoyed popular support. His army consisted of his old loyal followers, Roman legions in Britain, and bands of barbarian mercenaries.

In 293, Carausius was assassinated by one of his subordinates, Allectus, who declared himself emperor of Britannia and continued to defy central imperial authority in Rome. By that time, however, Western Roman Emperor Constantius Chlorus had had enough with the usurpers and had launched a successful invasion of Gaul, reclaiming much of the territory usurped by Carausius. Allectus and his supporters thus fled to Britain, where they established their defenses and held out against the "real" emperor's forces for three more years, until 296.

Constantius' reassertion of power in northern Gaul and Britain marked the end of the rebellion. After this incident, Emperor Diocletian introduced profound administrative changes to Britain to ensure that a single usurper could not challenge central authority again. Diocletian's measures brought relative stability to Britain for many decades (though, as we mentioned, the island was repeatedly subject to barbarian raids during the fourth century).

Three Usurpers

While 410 is generally considered the end of Roman rule over Britain, the decline of Roman influence on the island was a gradual process. As demonstrated, Roman Britannia faced many internal and external threats from the first to the fourth centuries, but it fared relatively well. The system of defenses established in Britain proved to be effective, and as long as a military presence was maintained, the barbarian invasions could not significantly undermine Roman control in the province.

In the late fourth century, however, the situation in Britannia began to deteriorate—in line with the overall situation in the Western Roman Empire. The empire was battling with migrating barbarian tribes forced to move westward into the territories of the Roman Empire during the Great Migration, as well as with economic crises, overextension, corruption, and civil wars between influential military leaders. All these factors played a role in the decline of Roman rule in Britain. It began when three consecutive usurpers, like Carausius almost a century before, challenged the authority of the imperial power.

In 383, Roman general Magnus Maximus, who had been assigned to Britain three years earlier, instigated the first revolt, declaring himself emperor. It is unclear whether this decision was Maximus' intention or his discontented soldiers pushed him to rebel, having felt disfavored due to the increasing number of foreign soldiers in the Roman armies. Whatever the case, Maximus, using his forces from Britain, quickly asserted himself in northern Gaul, making the city of Augusta Treverorum (modern-day Trier) his center. The same year, he defeated Western Emperor Gratian, who was killed in a skirmish in southeastern France, and marched to Italy to install himself as the "legitimate" emperor in Rome.

However, Maximus was stopped in his tracks by another Roman general, Flavius Bauto, who negotiated with him on behalf of Gratian's twelve-year-old successor, Valentinian II. In the end, Maximus was recognized as the "Augustus" of Gaul and Britannia, a rank that technically made him the equal of Valentinian and Theodosius, the ruler in the east. For the next few years, Maximus, now the recognized and legitimate Augustus of Gaul and Britannia, oversaw the defenses against the barbarians. He might have even campaigned against the Picts in the north.

Still, it appears that Maximus aspired to become Caesar as he tried to seize the opportunity four years later, taking his forces from Britannia and Gaul into northern Italia and attacking the city of Milan. Milan was the capital of the still young Emperor Valentinian II and his mother, Justina, who likely exerted much influence on her son and ruled from behind the scenes. They were forced to flee to the Greek city of Thessalonica, where they pleaded for Eastern Emperor Theodosius' help. Before Theodosius could properly assemble his forces and personally lead them to meet Maximus in battle, Maximus asserted his power in the other Italian cities. He prepared to defend against the impending response from the east at the Save River. The two armies finally met near the town of Siscia, in modern-day Croatia, where Theodosius routed Maximus' men. He captured the usurper and had him executed for treason, thus ending the first major rebellion from Britain in the late fourth century.

Emperor Theodosius I, who reigned as the Eastern Roman Emperor until his death in early 395, is regarded as one of the last great emperors before the fall of Rome in 476. In addition to defeating the usurper Magnum Maximus, he stabilized the mass migration of barbarians into the empire's territories relatively well, integrating many of them peacefully into Roman lands. Immediately after defeating Maximus, he reasserted control over Gaul and Britain and sent legions back to Hadrian's Wall to continue guarding against the barbarian attacks there.

In 392, another usurper, Eugenius, tried to challenge Theodosius' authority, but he ended the revolt two years later. In late 394, however, he began to suffer from a severe disease and died in January of the following year. His ten-year-old son, Honorius, succeeded him as emperor in the West, while his older brother, Arcadius, ruled in the

East. As Honorius was too young to rule, Stilicho, the husband of Theodosius' niece, assumed his regency.

During this time, Britain became increasingly isolated from the rest of the empire. The heightened barbarian invasions in the Roman lands made it difficult to establish communications. Stilicho may have at first campaigned in Britain against the Scots and the Picts, but sometime in 401 or 402, he requested the support of the British legions to fight against the barbarians in Gaul.

While barbarian raids in the more exposed parts of Britain continued, the situation became far worse in late 406, when large numbers of migrating barbarians made the crucial decision to cross the Rhine River—the border that separated Roman Gaul from the lands of the Germanic tribes. Barbarians had already migrated into Roman lands in numerous areas, and many were even offered positions in the Roman armies as *foederati* soldiers. However, crossing the Rhine, which most likely occurred on the last day of 406, marked a significant event. In contemporary chronicles, it is referred to as the event that brought about the widespread destruction of Roman towns in Gaul.

Roman legions were unable to stop the barbarians from crossing the river, as it had been frozen throughout winter. The defenses along the Rhine might also have been weakened, with soldiers sent to defend Italy from the more immediate Vandal, Visigothic, and Ostrogothic invasions that threatened the heart of the empire. Whatever the reasons for the crossing, towns such as Mainz, Rheims, Amiens, and many others were plundered by hordes of Alan, Alemanni, Burgundian, Saxon, Sarmatian, and Vandal tribes, putting further pressure on the Western Roman Empire. From this point, it became increasingly clear that it was impossible for Rome to salvage the situation.

The crossing of the Rhine held major importance for Roman Britannia. The citizens were clearly disenchanted by Emperor Honorius' decision to withdraw many soldiers from Britain, believing that the new wave of barbarian invasions also posed a threat to the island. Thus, in early 406, the people of Britain revolted again, electing their own emperor, a distinguished soldier named Marcus. He only lasted as a usurper for a few months before being overthrown in favor of another soldier—Gratian. It was likely the remaining Roman soldiers in Britain organized these rebellions, motivated by the fact that they had not been paid for years by Rome and wanting to take matters into their own hands.

Whatever the case, Gratian was also deposed in early 407, replaced by another man—Flavius Constantinus. Constantinus, or Constantine, was chosen in direct response to the barbarians crossing the Rhine, deduced from his actions after he assumed power in February of 407. Shortly after usurping power, he took the remaining British forces and crossed the English Channel to reach the city of Boulogne. This move was calculated to either directly fight the invading barbarians or reestablish contact with central imperial authority in Rome to pay his army. The second possibility is less likely as Constantine was technically revolting against Rome. It is unlikely the government would have met his demands unless he asserted himself by force.

Constantine's next course of action is even stranger. After arriving in Gaul and asserting himself in Boulogne, he entrusted control of a portion of his army to one of the commanders, Gerontius, and sent him to Spain. After reaching Spain, Gerontius rebelled against his former general, most likely in 409, and later turned back to face him, rousing Gaul's population against him. In an even stranger turn of events, around the same time, Constantine was briefly recognized by Emperor Honorius as co-emperor after he achieved some successes against the barbarians in Gaul.

Britain, on the other hand, was suffering heavily from renewed Saxon, Scot, and Pict attacks in 408-409, finding it increasingly difficult to repel them without a military presence. The British population in the cities, which had not received any help from the empire, decided to expel the Roman administrators—referring, most likely, to those that Constantine had put in place. This also took place in Gaul.

Our knowledge of this unexpected turn of events comes from Greek historian Zosimus, who lived in Constantinople in the late fifth century and wrote about the history of the Roman Empire from the mid-third to early fifth centuries. Zosimus blames this level of disenchantment on Constantine's rather unsuccessful rebellion and his inability to gain widespread support. He writes that the situation in Britannia certainly did not change for good with the rise of Constantine, who largely ignored the island and pushed his own agenda, which ended in complete failure. To complicate matters even more, in 411, after his attempted invasion of Italy, Constantine was captured and executed by Honorius, leading to a complete failure of Roman control in Gaul and Britain for a time.

The barbarian raids in Britain continued, however. According to Zosimus, the British population requested help from none other than Emperor Honorius. As it appears, this request was rejected by the emperor in 410. He was in no position to offer help to the British and told them to organize defenses on their own.

Nevertheless, it is unclear whether this correspondence between the British people and Honorius took place. For one, the cohesiveness of Roman communications at that time was questionable as the empire's administrative apparatus was failing due to increased barbarian invasions. In addition, Britannia was still technically rebelling against Honorius. (The British legions had proclaimed Marcus as their emperor in 406.) They may have thought that financial or military assistance from Rome was the only way to end the barbarian raids and were ready to declare their allegiance to the emperor. Since the description of these events in Zosimus' writings happens in the middle of his account of the ongoing situation in Italy, many historians even believe that he confused Britannia with the Italian province of Brettia.

Still, the year 410 marks the end of Roman control over Britain as Roman forces never again reinforced Britannia. Instead, the Romano-British population of the island had to find ways to adapt to the increasingly challenging circumstances, marking a new era in the history of Britain.

Chapter Two – The Arrival of the Anglo-Saxons in Britain

In 410, the Western Roman Empire was on the verge of collapse. It became increasingly difficult to deal with the waves of migratory barbarians into its territories, and the empire was struggling with an array of internal problems that significantly reduced its ability to rule effectively. As a result, the emperor had stopped caring for the farthest-lying provinces of the empire, unable to provide military and financial support and urging them to stand up for themselves in the face of barbarian threat. After being denied aid, Britain's population realized it was useless to rely on central imperial authority anymore. Britain was left alone and, if it wanted to survive, it had to survive alone. In this chapter, we will discuss the developments in post-Roman Britain, covering the gradual change of the status quo and the arrival of the eventual masters of the island—the Anglo-Saxons.

The Questions in Sub-Roman Britain

In the year 410, the situation in Britain was dire. Roman legions, stationed as garrisons to guard the frontier province, had been mostly withdrawn by the actions of Magnus Maximus in the late fourth century and by Stilicho and Constantine over the past decade. Whatever troops remained in Britain were likely of local Romano-Briton origin. As we mentioned, the population had also turned against the Roman magistrates in the cities. These people would have included civil servants who occupied higher positions in the Roman bureaucracy, though we do not know their names because of a lack of contemporary sources.

All in all, we can only speculate that the underlying theme of the chaotic situation was the following: the population of Britain, the majority of which were assimilated Britons, had rejected the notion of Roman authorities ruling over them, though they did not abandon their ways of life, which were still very Roman. Having decided to act independently, they must reorganize the government. Most importantly, they must also deal with barbarian incursions from all sides, including the Celtic Picts and Scots from the north and the west and the Germanic Saxons by sea.

Our knowledge of the events immediately following Honorius' refusal to help Britain depends largely on sources compiled from the late fifth century, which are profoundly criticized. Essentially, we know the least about the turn of events from the end of Roman rule in Britain to the arrival of the Anglo-Saxons and their rise to dominance, a period of about three or four decades.

The first source that tries to present a chronological account of this period is the work of Gildas, a British Christian monk who lived in the late fifth and early sixth centuries. His work *About the Ruin and Conquest of Britain* is mainly a religious book aimed at chastising the rulers of western Britain in the early sixth century. The historical account Gildas presents comprises one portion of the book and relies heavily on remembered and retold stories available to him. This means that the recounted events closer to the time of Gildas, i.e., the middle sixth century, should be considered more accurate than earlier ones. Other British sources of later times are partially or fully based on his work, so it is important to briefly discuss what we can infer from Gildas' account.

The historical inaccuracies in Gildas' account can be noticed right away, as he begins his story with the overthrow of usurper Magnum Maximus in 388, whom he refers to as the first truly independent ruler of Britain. According to Gildas, the Britons requested help from the imperial government three times after the overthrow of Maximus as the Picts and Scots continued their attacks. Gildas mentions that the Britons were told to, at first, build a turf wall as a defensive measure from the barbarians in the north. After the second appeal, they were told to build a stone wall. It is highly probable that this refers to the Roman-built defenses of the Antonine Wall and Hadrian's Wall and that his account serves to explain the existence of these walls in northern Britain.

It was Hadrian's Wall that was constructed first, beginning in 122. Work on the Antonine Wall, located farther north than Hadrian's Wall, began some twenty years later. Eventually, as we mentioned, the Antonine Wall was abandoned as it proved more difficult for the Romans to maintain, and Hadrian's Wall became the northernmost frontier of Roman Britannia. However, the construction of these defenses is by no means connected to the overthrow of Magnus Maximus or the period that Gildas talks about in his work. Gildas' account also completely omits Constantine's later rebellion, though it is unlikely the source that provided him with the story of Magnus Maximus would have left this out.

What Gildas rightly mentions is that a third appeal for help was made to a Roman general called Agitius, but this also produced no response from the imperial authority. Gildas mentions that, after this, as the Picts and Scots' attacks intensified, an "unlucky tyrant" (*infaustus tyrannus*) of Britain sought advice from his council and invited the Saxons to help against these invasions.

Gildas' account is used by the early eighth-century English monk Bede in his *Ecclesiastical History of the English People*. Bede adapts this history and does not largely diverge from Gildas' narrative, fixing the date of the Saxons' arrival in 447. There is no way of knowing whether this is the date of the first Saxon mercenaries' arrival, but the general chronological order of the story after their arrival in Britain matches Gildas' account.

We also have the account from the *History of the Britons*, which was originally attributed to a Welsh monk named Nennius, who lived in the ninth century. Nennius' story, however, is heavily influenced by the fact that he wrote as a monk under King Merfyn of the Welsh Kingdom of Gwynedd. Many details might have been changed accordingly. Evidence about the events of early fifth-century Britain can also be found in the *Anglo-Saxon Chronicle*, compiled in the later ninth century. Still, the identification of exact dates is very difficult.

Vortigern, Hengist, and Horsa

From these accounts, we can derive the basic outline of the early post-Roman history of Britain. After Britain's inability to gain support from the failing Roman Empire, the raiding Celtic tribes, especially from the north, put increasing pressure on the Romano-Briton population. This persisted for some time before those who still held authority in the former Roman province, be it a council or the "unlucky tyrant" referred to by Gildas, called for help from the next best option—the Saxons. The Britons decided to invite Saxon mercenaries to fight off the Pict and Scot raiders, which led to more and more Saxon fighters arriving in Britain.

But who exactly was in charge of Britain after the expulsion of Roman magistrates? This is a question that needs to be answered before we discuss the rate and degree of Saxon migration to Britain.

Even though Britannia was no longer connected to the central imperial authority in Rome, its way of life and social organization was still very much Roman. The Britons still regarded themselves as rightful members of Roman civilization. The expulsion of imperial authorities was simply a sign of protest to the emperor who cared little for his subjects, not a complete rejection of Rome.

One aspect of social life that had been present in Britain from the time of the Romans was the local councils, which were established to govern the Britain civitates more effectively. In Zosimus' account of Honorius' alleged response to the plea of the Britons, the emperor seemed to address the cities of Britain. This indicates that the local governance system was still prominent in 410. There is little reason to suspect that it would be completely abandoned afterward.

Similarly, there is a high chance that those who had supposedly asked the emperor for help were members of the higher classes, perhaps the landed nobility whose estates, located outside of the walled cities, were more threatened by the barbarian invasions. It is also likely that this circle of local administrators and nobles governed Britain in the absence of a clear ruler after the revolt in 406.

However, desperate times call for desperate measures, and the Britons likely searched for individual figures to lead them out of their desperation in the early fifth century. In times of great crisis, the Roman Republic itself would grant almost unrestricted power to a single individual—the dictator—who would be elected for a certain term by the Senate to deal with the crisis. It is thus likely that the "unlucky tyrant," who, according to Gildas, resorted to calling the Saxons for aid against the Picts and the Scots, was a real historical figure.

In Gildas' account, this figure is aided by a council, which might refer to one of the local councils from the original organization of Roman civitates in Britain. Still, as Gildas refers to him as *tyrannus*, it seems he was not elected to this position. The fact that Gildas refers to him as "unlucky" likely signifies that after his decision, Britain was swarmed by the immigrating Saxons and forced to go to war. Thus, we can infer from Gildas' account that, though a single man held considerable power in immediate post-Roman Britain, the old local council organization was still very prominent.

Bede, the author of the *Ecclesiastical History of the English People*, expands on Gildas' account of the tyrant. He identifies him as a man named Vortigern, which translates from Celtic as "high king." This does not necessarily mean Vortigern was the king who ruled over all the territories in former Roman Britannia. Nevertheless, he held some power and influence in early fifth-century Britain. Crucially, Bede also mentions the names of the first invited Saxon leaders, brothers Hengist and Horsa. According to Bede, they were the first chieftains of the Saxon barbarians who eventually also fought against the Britons, Vortigern included.

Illustration of Bede.
https://commons.wikimedia.org/wiki/File:E-codices_bke-0047_001v_medium_(cropped).jpg

Later sources expand on this account, saying that the chieftain brothers landed near Ebbsfleet in Kent. The small force they brought was successful at first in defeating the Picts and was paid by the Britons. After witnessing their success, Vortigern believed that the strategy was working and asked the brothers to bring back more of their tribesmen to settle in Kent and fight. Seeing the chaotic situation in Britain, Hengist and Horsa sent word back to their homeland, noting that the Britons were still very disorganized and requested more reinforcements. According to the chronicles, they intended to betray their employers.

The Saxon soldiers brought their families and settled in southeastern Britain. Nennius writes that Vortigern fell in love with Hengist's daughter, who had come to Britain. Blinded with love, the British ruler told Hengist that he would do anything in exchange for his daughter's hand. The Saxon chieftain requested control of Kent, which was granted to him in due time.

Sometime after this, conflict broke out between the Saxons and the Britons, the exact reasons for which are unknown. Gildas says that the first part of the conflict culminated in the Battle of Mount Badon, an exceptionally bloody battle in which the Britons achieved victory and beat the Saxons back to Kent, establishing a truce.

There is a lot to unpack in this account of Vortigern, Hengist, and Horsa. First, though all early chronicles mention Hengist and Horsa as the first Saxon leaders who crossed the English Channel to fight as mercenaries for the Britons, historians hold the consensus that they were not real figures. The details about them do not appear in Gildas' account, the earliest compilation of retold and remembered stories by his contemporaries. Bede's and Nennius' accounts, as well as the *Anglo-Saxon Chronicle*, say that Hengist and Horsa trace their genealogy to Woden, or Odin—the most revered god in Norse mythology and an important deity in early Germanic pagan beliefs. Their names, "Hengist" and "Horsa," are also Old English for "stallion" and "horse."

The combination of all these factors, including their alliterative names, mythical genealogy, and the lack of historical evidence from closer to their time, makes it unclear whether they really existed. For that matter, the same can be said about Vortigern. Still, it is far more probable one powerful individual among the Britons invited the Saxons to come and fight as mercenaries against the Picts and the Scots immediately after the collapse of the Roman order.

We can reasonably infer from all these accounts, however, that by the late fifth century, profound changes had already begun to take place in post-Roman Britain. The local Romano-Briton population had called for aid from the Germanic Saxons, who had begun coming in increasing numbers and settling in Kent. By the time of Gildas, a conflict between the Saxons and the Britons had already broken out and been resolved.

Reconstructing the Anglo-Saxon Settlement

Since the textual evidence we have of immediate post-Roman Britain is not enough to reconstruct the history of the Saxons' arrival, we must look at material evidence that dates back to the fifth century to confirm these sometimes-conflicting accounts. From this evidence, we can deduce that a significant cultural and linguistic shift took place in Britain in the mid-fifth century that, in a way, supports the narratives of the chroniclers we discussed.

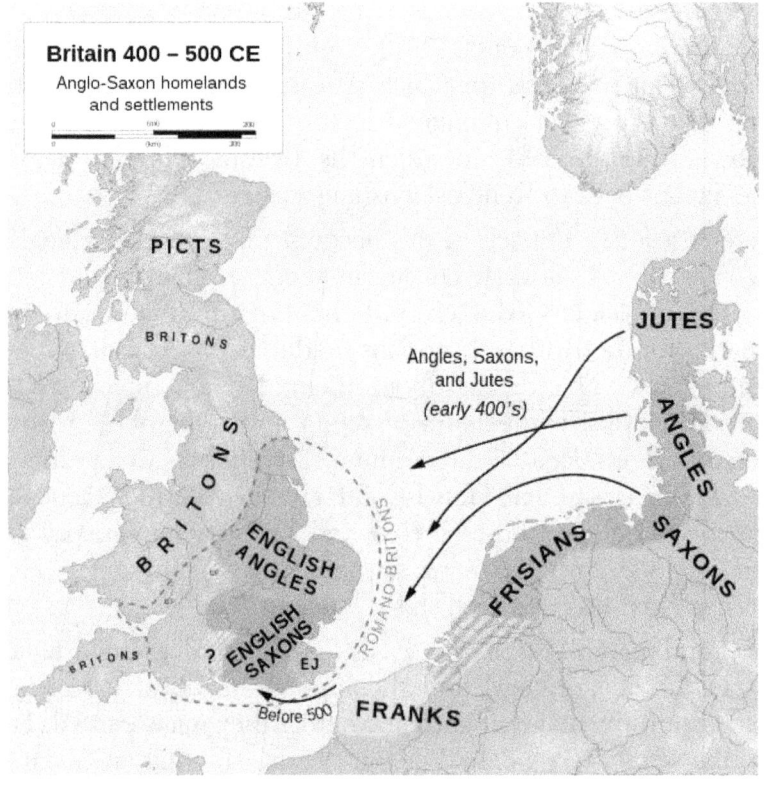

Patterns of Anglo-Saxon migration to England.
mbartelsm, CC BY-SA 3.0 <https://creativecommons.org/licenses/by-sa/3.0>, via Wikimedia Commons; https://commons.wikimedia.org/wiki/File:Anglo-Saxon_Homelands_and_Settlements.svg

By the time of the decline of Roman rule, most of the British population spoke two languages—a Brittonic version of Latin or British Celtic. Latin was obviously brought to the island by the Romans and was the de-facto language of the province just as it was in the empire. British Celtic, on the other hand, was the original language of the Britons, who maintained a strong link to their Celtic origins and did not give up speaking the language even as they were conquered and dominated by a completely different civilization. This can be explained by the relative tolerance the Romans showed toward the cultures and languages of the people they conquered, as we discussed earlier.

In post-Roman Britain, it appears that language played a vital role in identifying the ethnic or cultural makeup of the society. The primarily Saxon, Angle, and Jute immigrants that began arriving in Britain in the fifth century brought their own dialects of Germanic languages. These dialects eventually merged into Old English, an ancestor of the modern English language used to write this book. In the following few centuries, as the influence of these Germanic migrants grew, Old English appears to have become the dominant language in eastern, southern, and central Britain, while British Celtic was driven to the edges of the old Roman province.

By the eighth century, Celtic was spoken in Wales, Ireland, and Scotland—the areas less affected by the Anglo-Saxon migration. It was also spoken in the most southwestern areas of Britain—most famously in Cornwall, where Cornish (a version of Celtic) continued to be prominently spoken until the eighteenth century despite centuries of Anglicization. Celtic also persevered in northwestern France in the region of Brittany, where many Britons migrated after the arrival of the Saxons.

Though Old English has some Celtic influences, it has few words of Celtic origin. This is a unique phenomenon. While the Germanic tribes penetrated deep into the territories of the Roman Empire—for example, into Gaul, Iberia, Italia, and even North Africa—they largely adopted local languages. Thus, key questions arise when examining the emergence of Old English as the dominant language of post-Roman Britain. Was it the result of a decisive military takeover and the forceful assertion of a completely new order that might have included, for example, the prohibition of British Celtic? Or, did it result from the emergence of an Old English-speaking elite whose language became more prestigious for commoners to speak over time, at the expense of their native languages?

The idea of the Anglo-Saxons' military domination is partially supported by the accounts of Gildas and Bede, which mention conflicts breaking out between the immigrants and the locals soon after the collapse of Roman rule in Britain.

The second hypothesis is somewhat supported by textual evidence. The *Anglo-Saxon Chronicle* mentions that the early Saxons killed many local British leaders in their encounters in the second half of the fifth century. According to Nennius' *History of the Britons*, Hengist invited Vortigern and other British leaders to a feast to celebrate peace, where Hengist had instructed his men to hide knives in their attire and kill the unsuspecting Britons. Many British leaders (who, if Nennius is correct, were the remaining nobility) were slain. Vortigern, who was spared, was forced to give up control of eastern and central British lands to the Saxons. This account is repeated in Geoffrey of Monmouth's *History of the Kings of Britain*, though the reliability of this source is also doubted. Still, it appears that the Saxons somehow eliminated the high-ranking local British nobility and asserted themselves in their place.

According to this theory, this resulted in a dramatic shift in the political order. Many Britons would have been influenced to adopt the language of the Saxons, as it may have given them more advantages or been required by the new leadership. Nevertheless, the language shift that took place in post-Roman Britain was gradual, as every language shift is. It must have taken place over several generations as the Anglo-Saxon domination of England became more prominent.

Archeological evidence supports the general claim that the Anglo-Saxon settlement occurred in Britain from east to west. The clearest evidence of this is the distribution of Anglo-Saxon burial sites, which are distinguishable from Romano-British sites. For example, Mucking, an archeological site located in southeastern Essex, contains a large cemetery where both Romano-British and Anglo-Saxon-style burial sites have been discovered, and the latter are more numerous.

Mucking is believed to have been a British settlement before it was abandoned and inhabited by the Anglo-Saxons, possibly even earlier than the traditional date of their migration to Britain in the 420s or 430s. The proximity of this site to other Romano-British settlements and the diffusion of Saxon graves with local graves suggests that the Germanic inhabitants of the place may have been *foederati* soldiers in the late fourth or early fifth century. Mucking also contains more than two hundred Saxon-style buildings, called *Grubenhaus*, a type of small pit-house. Generally, the earliest Anglo-Saxon sites have been discovered in the eastern parts of England, all the way north to the River Humber. This also partially confirms the account of their settlement patterns in the late fifth and early sixth centuries.

The fact that the earliest Anglo-Saxons were mercenaries can be quite reasonably reconfirmed by the discovery of belt fittings that bear ornamental carvings, including animal carvings that resemble Germanic styles. They have been found in an array of sites, such as Mucking, the late Roman burial sites at Winchester, and even France.

Though these belt fittings are reminiscent of the Germanic style and taste, they were most likely used by both Saxon and local Romano-British soldiers. Late Roman pottery also bears a Germanic style, so much so that the pots have been attributed to a distinct Romano-Saxon style, indicating a high degree of contact between the two cultures. It is apparent that Roman Britannia started to produce pots with Germanic decorations as early as the late fourth century. This indicates a demand for such goods, pointing to the close relationship the late Roman Britannia had with the Saxon culture.

Thus, there is linguistic, cultural, and material evidence of Saxon presence in Britain by the mid-fifth century that supports contemporary literary sources. People of Germanic origin populated parts of eastern Britain, especially the region of Kent, and very likely arrived there as *foederati* mercenaries. It appears that they lived somewhat separate from the rest of the local British society. In time, more Saxons migrated to the shores of Britain and, whether through warfare, domination of the Briton elites, or cultural assimilation, asserted their control over the local population. What came next was a profound transformation of the social, cultural, and political landscape of post-Roman Britain. By the mid-sixth century, the Anglo-Saxons were master of Britain.

Chapter Three – The Birth of Anglo-Saxon England

In this chapter, we will look at the period following the Anglo-Saxon settlement in post-Roman Britain, which includes profound socio-political transformations. As we saw in the previous chapter, the events following the Anglo-Saxons' arrival in Britain that caused them to become the dominant force by the middle of the sixth century are shrouded in mystery. But, by the late sixth century, when Pope Gregory I decided to send a mission to Britain, the Anglo-Saxons had already established their state-like formations, based fundamentally on their native tribal structures. As we will see, the transformation from these forms of social and political organization to a better-developed kingship was aided by the introduction of Christianity, a similarity that Anglo-Saxon England shared with Early Middle Ages Western Europe.

Origins of Anglo-Saxon Kingdoms

In whatever way the Saxon immigrants came to dominate the local Romano-Briton population, it would take them centuries to form what could be referred to as "kingdoms." This was due to fundamental differences between the socio-cultural organizations of the Romano-Briton civilization and the Saxons' Germanic way of life.

At the time of the Great Migration, the social organization of the Saxons, Angles, and Jutes was still in the form of tribal chiefdoms. These chiefdoms had a strict hierarchy, with a successful military leader, or chieftain, at the top. A chieftain would hold almost undisputed authority and executive power, though he would often consult with a council of elders or experienced warriors for advice on important matters. He would often oversee not only his tribal village but also several other surrounding villages, mostly based on his military power. Thus, the chieftain's status, though based on kinship and mostly hereditary, would sometimes be the subject of contention between the different tribes or communities that made up a chiefdom.

Each community that served the chieftain would be bound to him by a series of aspects, most prominently sacred oaths with which they swore their loyalty. This was rooted in their pagan belief systems. Chieftains also collected different types of tribute as a testament to their subordinates' loyalty.

Overall, the social organization of Germanic chiefdoms was very different from that of the Romano-Briton civilization, which was far more based on clearly defined socio-economic roles, centrally appointed bureaucracy for administration, and distinctions between urban and rural classes.

As the Anglo-Saxons and Jutes began arriving in Britain in large numbers by the end of the fifth century, they continued to practice their native forms of social organization and patterns of settlement, which included the formation of small chiefdoms. This is not to say that their communities excluded the local Romano-Britons, however, or that they did not take over the existing settlement patterns.

One of the major pieces of evidence for this is the adoption and modification of topographical names. This is apparent in Kent, for example, which would emerge as one of the major kingdoms in later Anglo-Saxon England. The name was derived from its old Latin name, *Cantium,* with its center at the old Latin *Durovernum Cantiacorum,* which means "stronghold of the *Cantiaci* (Kentish) people." Eventually, the Anglo-Saxons would adopt and modify the name into Old English as *Cantwaraburg,* from which stems the modern name of Canterbury.

Romano-Briton political units, whether civitates, sub-provinces, or small communities, were largely preserved by the Anglo-Saxons in different areas, as well. One example is the Kingdom of Northumbria, which achieved its relatively stable form of social and political organization in the seventh century. Its boundaries closely resemble those of the late Roman administrative unit, Britannia Secunda, introduced by the reforms of Diocletian. Of course, Northumbria is a reference to a geographic demarcation—north of the Humber River. This referencing system was increasingly used in the Middle Anglo-Saxon period, from the late seventh century onward. The city of York, the center of the Roman sub-province, retained its importance in the later Anglo-Saxon kingdom, as well.

The Anglo-Saxon tribal chiefdoms varied in size and importance, and the emerging kingdoms absorbed many of them to form larger political units. In addition to Bede's *Ecclesiastical History*, we know of them from the Tribal Hidage—a unique list compiled during the seventh to the ninth centuries that mentions the names of thirty-five tribes and assigns "hides" to each one of them. A hide was an old English unit of measurement for land. After the Norman Conquest of 1066, it appears to have been 120 acres, but it was most likely a much smaller unit during the Anglo-Saxon period. In any case, the Tribal Hidage was most likely compiled by a powerful leader to accept tributes from his subordinates based on their size and productive capacity. It is thus likely that larger or more powerful chiefdoms asserted their dominance over the smaller and weaker tribes, exacting tribute in exchange for protection, among other reasons.

We should also consider the social, rather than spatial, organization that led to large-scale political transformation. Bede, for example, clearly refers to the larger kingdoms that existed during his time by the name of their peoples instead of their lands—the Mercians, for example. This suggests that social relationships that stemmed from the old values of hierarchical kinship remained just as important as the distribution of different tribes in certain territories. The smaller tribes or chiefdoms that made up the larger kingdoms thus continued to recognize and acknowledge their leader, or "king," in exchange for his protection. This is not unique to the Anglo-Saxons. It was the prevalent form of sociopolitical organization in Early Middle Ages Europe, where the prominence and power of war chieftains and their chiefdoms led to the rise of clear political boundaries.

Though military power was most important, after a while the "royal" lineage of a single family would have accumulated enough support and legitimacy to press its claims to control of a certain territory. Those who inhabited this territory would often support the claimant, even if his authority was temporarily challenged by a usurper from a rival faction or chiefdom.

Thus, the origins of kingship in Anglo-Saxon England lay in fundamental relationships between tribal communities and distinguished war leaders who accrued support, power, wealth, and prestige over time, eventually inheriting the position based on the successes of their predecessors. The importance of this inherently tribal understanding of social relations is affirmed when we trace the etymology of the word "king" (*cyning* in Old English), which derives from "kin" (*cynn*).

Reconstructing the exact relationships between the early Anglo-Saxon chiefdoms is very difficult, not only because of the lack of evidence but also because such relationships are always complex. There is no reason to suspect that the emigrating Angles, Saxons, and Jutes were mostly peaceful with each other. They were different peoples with different leaders who, as we will see later, settled in different parts of Britain with different interests.

A tribal leader could gain power that would raise his prestige as a chieftain in many ways, not just through warfare and military domination of a rival chiefdom or tribe. In a small area that was populated with rival small-scale chiefdoms, conflicts over resources, above all, were bound to happen. Chieftains might also strengthen their position through intermarriages between the tribes' elite, which would improve relations between the two. They could also simply negotiate the patronage of a smaller or weaker tribe if it was in need.

Kingship thus emerged from the merging of small tribes and chiefdoms, which could happen for various reasons. As in other parts of the world, kingship in Anglo-Saxon England had multiple tiers. The notion of "over-kingship," something that Bede identifies by the word *imperium* (rule of the emperor) instead of the word *regnum* (rule of the king), certainly existed. Naturally, some kings were more powerful and prominent and exerted their influence over others. This was a larger-scale version of the domination of one chieftain over the others but was much less rare and much more unstable.

For example, Bede refers to King Ethelbert of Kent as the third figure to exert "over-kingship" over the other lesser kingdoms in southern England. Before him, Bede mentions King Ælle of the South Saxons and King Ceawlin of the West Saxons, who reigned in the late fifth to early and late sixth centuries, respectively. Bede again says that these figures were kings of different peoples—South Saxons and West Saxons—suggesting that the territorial boundaries between them were not yet firmly in place.

In conclusion, based on the material and textual evidence of fifth, sixth, and early seventh-century Britain, several things can be assumed about the emergence of kingship in Anglo-Saxon Britain. The first Anglo-Saxon kings of Britain emerged from a complex network of tribal interrelations that favored chiefdoms with prominent chieftains as their leaders. Early chieftains emerged either through military dominance or negotiations and alliances between different chiefdoms, resulting in a fluid political system. Some chiefdoms integrated local civil and social structures into their rule to bolster their legitimacy and gain more power.

Everything from the deaths of prominent leaders to the outcomes of battles and inter-tribal "royal" marriages may have contributed to shifts in power between the chiefdoms of Britain early on, which we must imagine were frequent. Undoubtedly, some chiefdoms declined soon after gaining power, while others persisted thanks to the intricacies they developed to maintain loyalty and support, such as the payment of tributes and military service.

After these relationships became more permanent and rooted over decades, we can more reliably call a former chieftain, who had perhaps inherited leadership, a king. And, as it appears, by the late sixth century, these developments were already well underway when the papal mission arrived in the domains of the Anglo-Saxons to spread Christianity.

Early Anglo-Saxon Society

A term often used to refer to the organization of Anglo-Saxon rule in England from the sixth century is "heptarchy," or the "rule of the seven." This term implies that seven dominant kingdoms existed in Anglo-Saxon England, whose dominance became especially prominent during the seventh century.

When we describe the political organization of Early Middle Ages England as a heptarchy, it is important to understand that the dynamics between the kingdoms were constantly evolving. It is likely that clear differences between the kingdoms, such as established borders, did not exist and were always fluctuating.

The seven kingdoms of the heptarchy included Wessex, Sussex, Essex, Kent, East Anglia, Mercia, and Northumbria. Wessex, East Anglia, Mercia, and Northumbria would eventually overpower the other three, though their rise and decline is a complex matter we will discuss later.

The kingdoms of the Anglo-Saxon heptarchy.
https://commons.wikimedia.org/wiki/File:Anglo-Saxon_Heptarchy.jpg

Importantly, these kingdoms can best be distinguished by the ethnocultural groups that dominated them. The Saxon migrants of Britain mostly organized themselves in Wessex, Sussex, and Essex, evident in the naming of their domains. The Angles, on the other hand, settled in the northern and central-eastern parts of the island in Northumbria, East Anglia, and Mercia. Kent, which included the areas first settled by the "Saxon" warriors invited by the Romano-Briton rulers, was most prominently inhabited by the Jutes.

These Germanic groups were technically different when we consider their ethnic and cultural characteristics. They had all dwelled in different regions of continental Europe, concentrated separately in northern Germany and Jutland. However, they still shared many similarities, especially in the eyes of the Romano-Britons, who conveniently called them all Saxons when they first arrived as pseudo-*foederati* soldiers. At least, they were far more different from the locals and their mix of Celtic and Roman culture than from each other.

Thus, when these Germanic groups eventually replaced the Romano-Britons as masters of Britain, they needed a term to distinguish themselves from their counterparts that still inhabited northern Germany and Jutland. Since their Germanic dialects had coalesced to the point that a distinct language—Old English—had been developed, it was logical that the most obvious distinction should be linguistic. Thus, they used the term "Anglo-Saxon" to refer to the Germanic inhabitants of Britain, as opposed to "Saxon," which referred to the continental group. By the eighth century, when the term began to be used extensively in this context, the Angle, Saxon, and Jute tribes that had originally migrated to Britain had assimilated with and dominated the local Britons.

Some rulers of the kingdoms of the heptarchy would also be considered over-kings, as their domains contained several sub-kingdoms or sub-provinces, each with less powerful rulers but a clearly stated identity. Such polities included, most importantly, Bernicia and Deira, which covered most of the Kingdom of Northumbria; Lindsey and Middle Anglia, part of the Kingdom of Mercia; and Hwicce and Gewisse in the Kingdom of Wessex.

The arrival of Anglo-Saxons and the gradual establishment of their domains profoundly affected more than just the political situation of post-Roman Britain. The immigrants brought a unique culture and way of life that was integrated with the remnants of the Romano-Briton culture, giving birth to a completely new society. While some social structures and lifestyles were maintained or modified, others—especially the belief systems and overall culture of the region—were profoundly shaken up.

The imposition of Anglo-Saxon rule and the subsequent growth of chiefdoms into kingdoms meant that they must reorganize socially and economically, above all. The old tribal Anglo-Saxon lifestyle, based on warfare and sustained by constant plundering and raiding, could not be maintained for long. Better and more reliable sources of income were necessary if the chieftains, now princes and kings, were to maintain their power and keep the political status quo. Many of them decided to revive the agriculture-based economy of Roman Britain, some with more success than others.

The main producers of agricultural goods—and thus the contributors to the economy—were no longer servile peasants who worked for a small group of elites on their lavish estates, however. Instead, the main practitioners of agriculture were the ceorls, free members of the lowest social class in the Anglo-Saxon kingdoms. The ceorls, or churls, were essentially free peasants, practicing communal agriculture while also paying regular tax to the nobles. This class of free peasantry was maintained until the advent of feudal manorialism in Europe, when the ceorls' freedoms were gradually reduced by the landed nobility in the High Middle Ages. By the late seventh century, for example, Anglo-Saxon nobles began to possess substantial estates housing several peasant families, which were occasionally taxed a fixed amount in exchange for protection by the nobility.

The granting of lands by kings was more common with distinguished members of society, such as good warriors, loyal nobles, or bishops. Again, this was done to increase the kings' influence and power. They hoped to not only build good relationships with their subordinates and guarantee their support in the future but also buy services for themselves. Esteemed warriors, for example, were granted sizeable estates by kings so that they would fight for them and their descendants.

The domestic economy began to increase as the social and political roles in Anglo-Saxon England became more fixed. With it came the development of early industries and the rise of exports by local merchants, who mostly traded with the Franks across the English Channel. The relative establishment of borders between the different kingdoms made the defense and oversight of trade routes and networks more feasible, increasing domestic exchange and the production of goods such as pottery, metals, and woolen cloth. These goods were also exported to foreign markets in the early stages of development.

As Early Middle Ages Europe recovered from the complete socio-economic collapse that had followed the fall of the Western Roman Empire, global trading networks were also being re-established, and Anglo-Saxon kingdoms were part of it. Archeological evidence points to the existence of exotic goods like silks and lavish vessels from Byzantium, elephant ivory, and Arabian incense in Early Anglo-Saxon England.

The Anglo-Saxons' connection with European civilizations is evidenced by the presence of Byzantine gold coins dated to the seventh century. Early Anglo-Saxon gold coinage was also developed by then, influenced by the Frankish Merovingian style, with depictions of rulers' busts on one side and symbols, such as crosses, on the other. The earliest Anglo-Saxon coins were minted at major trading sites, referred to as wics, such as in London, York, or Ipswich. Wics would increasingly develop in coastal areas from the middle of the seventh century.

At this stage, coins minted in Anglo-Saxon England did not correspond to European standards, especially the fixed rates and regulated minting present in the Byzantine Empire. Still, the fact that the Anglo-Saxons switched from a gold to a silver-based economy in the late seventh century and began minting their own silver coins indicates some level of cohesion with continental societies, like the Franks, who probably influenced this shift.

From Briton Christianity to Anglo-Saxon Paganism

Importantly, Roman Britain had been Christian before the Anglo-Saxons' migration in the fifth century, though the role of Christianity had certainly diminished with the arrival of Anglo-Saxon paganism as the major belief system. One must imagine that this religious distinction was one of the biggest differences between the local Romano-Britons and the Anglo-Saxons. It could have been one of the main drivers of conflict between the two groups, in whatever form that transpired.

Before the end of Roman rule in Britain in the early fifth century, British bishops had been actively involved in the religious affairs of the empire, attending several councils during the fourth century. While they were not present at the First Council of Nicaea in 325, which came to regulate many of the doctrinal issues of early Christianity, they were present at Arles in 314, at Serdica in 343, and at Ariminum in 359. This is even more impressive considering that Britain had been one of the last provinces where Roman rule was consolidated and was farthest from the birthplace of Christianity. The remoteness of the region meant that the local polytheistic Celtic belief system was a major competitor to Christianity.

Despite the smaller size of the Church in late Roman Britain, some religious figures stood out. A theologian from the British Isles in the late fourth to early fifth centuries, Pelagius was a prominent figure of the early Church, alongside such contemporaries as Augustine of Hippo. At this time, many of the central questions in Christianity were still being identified and clarified, and there were several different versions of the religion.

Pelagius was active in the decades after the establishment of the Nicene Creed that sought to introduce doctrinal universality and resolve many of the issues of the Church in the early fourth century. He was the proponent of a theological understanding of Christianity called Pelagianism. Pelagius, alongside his disciple Celestius, argued against the belief that humans were inherently sinful, tainted by original sin, and instead believed that God had granted humans a degree of free will to choose between good or evil, including the capacity to sin. For these views, he was condemned by several consecutive councils held in Africa. (He had moved there to escape from his original dwelling in Rome, which was sacked in 410.)

Pelagius' principal opponent was St. Augustine of Hippo, who eventually became one of the most important theologians of Christianity. In 418, Pelagianism was declared heretical, and Pelagius was excommunicated from the Church, though a version of this belief system continued to be prominent in some regions, including post-Roman Britain.

In fact, in the late 420s, Bishop Germanus of Auxxere from Gaul was sent to Britain to deal with the rising prominence of Pelagianism in the British clergy. (Germanus also led the Britons in a successful battle against the barbarians.) The *Life of Saint Germanus,* which recounts the story of his visit to Britain, provides insights into post-Roman Britain's socio-political situation near the beginning of the Anglo-Saxon migration.

In short, there is good evidence that Christianity had been firmly established in Roman Britain by the time of the pagan Anglo-Saxons' arrival. Although the importance of Christianity would gradually decline from the middle of the fifth to the end of the sixth century, Christian communities nevertheless persevered in parts of post-Roman Britain, especially in the western part of the island.

During this period characterized by the Germanic societies' rise in prominence, it is logical that their belief system became the most important. Anglo-Saxon paganism is a religion we know little about, partially due to the lack of any written sources composed by its followers. What we know of the pagan beliefs and practices of Anglo-Saxons comes from the later writings of Christian authors such as Bede—who, of course, held quite negative views of them.

The Anglo-Saxons certainly did not use the word "pagan" to describe their religious belief system. This was a Latin pejorative word used by Early Middle Ages writers to express their disapproval of the un-Christian religion. Sometimes, pagans were also called "heathens" in early Anglo-Saxon Old English, a word that has retained its negative connotation. Interestingly, the Anglo-Saxons would themselves refer to the Viking invaders of Britain in the eighth and ninth centuries as heathens.

Anglo-Saxon paganism was a polytheistic belief system. Though the practice of paganism had several distinctions based on the regional distribution of Germanic tribes, its overarching system was shared by the Germanic peoples. It shared many similarities with other Germanic beliefs that would eventually develop into systems we know far more about, like the Norse mythology of Scandinavian peoples. For example, the pagan Anglo-Saxon deity of whom we have the most evidence is Woden, who shared many similarities with Odin, the chief deity in the Norse pantheon. Many places throughout England seem to bear his name, such as the village of Woodnesborough, or "Woden's Borough," and Wansdyke, or "Woden's Dyke," a defensive structure in western England. Woden is also mentioned as the ancestor of the royal families of Kent, Mercia, East Anglia, and Wessex, which can be explained as an attempt to legitimize royal rule.

In addition to a pantheon of gods and goddesses, the Anglo-Saxons also believed in other deities and supernatural beings, such as spirits and ghosts. Their rituals—like animal sacrifice, which was very prominent—were directed by priests and generally sought divine favor or luck from the deities.

We have every reason to suspect that aspects of the pagan Anglo-Saxon belief system were closely interlinked with everyday life, including areas such as agriculture, military affairs, and laws. Some characteristics of Anglo-Saxon society and other early Germanic societies, such as the role of storytelling and general assembly, can also be explained by the important role of pagan priests and religious practices.

In turn, as Anglo-Saxon chieftains began to increase their power after coming to post-Roman Britain, transforming their domains into "kingdoms," it is possible they were challenged by the priestly class. While the "political" leaders of the early Anglo-Saxon society were tribal chieftains who held military power, the priests held the same role in the "socio-cultural" context. If this is true, conversion to Christianity would have offered the tribal leaders and chieftains the ability to gain more influence in religious affairs. They could exert control over the Christian clergy, thus bringing an aspect of Anglo-Saxon social life further under their power. Therefore, it is necessary to view the emergence of Anglo-Saxon kingship as inherently interconnected with their Christianization.

Christianity and Anglo-Saxons

The conversion of Anglo-Saxons to Christianity marks a turning point in their history. It held paramount importance not only for the local population and the kings but also for the rest of the Christian world, which had experienced many setbacks with the fall of the Western Roman Empire. The migrating hordes of pagan barbarians that had overwhelmed the socio-political structures of the empire had also undermined Christianity in the fifth century.

The declining prominence of Christianity as a religion in provinces such as Gaul, Iberia, and Britannia, and to a lesser extent in North Africa and Italia, led to the development of another set of problems. Many practices previously kept by Christian clergy, like record-keeping or education, continued to decline, leading to a vacuum of knowledge in post-Roman Western Europe after 476. For example, it would take a long time for the tradition of learning, previously heavily tied to Christianity, to reemerge as a widespread aspect of European public life in the Late Middle Ages.

More importantly, Christianity had also been a source of legitimacy for late Roman rulers. Since the late fourth century, the Roman emperors had been Christians, a status that had become synonymous with Roman emperorship. This became apparent in the political chaos that ensued after 476. The barbarian invaders, as in England, had begun assimilating local populations. They began to call themselves kings, introducing a completely different culture and way of life that dominated the old Roman civilization and traditions. Overall, this was a decentralized process.

Who were the local populations to look up to in such times of crisis? Some pointed to the emperor in Constantinople. Despite the fall of Rome, the Eastern Roman (Byzantine) Empire had persevered, still the largest and the most powerful political entity in the known world in the fifth century. It was "Roman" by all means, with a Christian emperor and way of life characteristic of the Roman Empire.

The self-proclaimed "kings" of the Franks, Visigoths, Vandals, Ostrogoths, Burgundians, and other former barbarian peoples recognized the importance of the Eastern Roman Emperor. They also began to adopt some of the practices and titles of the old Western emperors to legitimize their rule. Some, like King Theodoric the Great of the Ostrogothic Kingdom, waged wars on neighboring rulers to strengthen their positions as the most prominent kings in post-Roman Europe. Nevertheless, these barbarian kings were never recognized by Byzantium as legitimate rulers, let alone as equals of the emperor in Constantinople.

Eastern writers denounced their kingship and lamented the days when the western half of the empire had been as strong. Many imagined a world in which the Eastern Roman Empire reestablished control over the lost provinces in Europe. This was perhaps best achieved by Emperor Justinian in the middle of the sixth century when he reconquered parts of Italy, North Africa, and Iberia for a time.

However, perhaps it was clear from the beginning that there was no way for the Eastern Roman Empire to exercise control over the old provinces of the West. The scale of the socio-political turmoil was way too large for that to have been possible. The barbarian invasions had disrupted communication channels between the East and the West, where, as we mentioned, any remnant of central administration had disappeared by the late fifth century. All in all, as the future of Europe and the old territories of the Western Roman Empire seemed uncertain, the Eastern Roman Empire could not afford to resolve the turmoil of the West.

Still, an individual or institution needed to reimpose order to keep the emerging barbarian kingdoms in check and provide a solution to the chaos that had ensued after the fall of Rome. And, in due time, the Roman Catholic Church would take this mantle. It had suffered just as much with the fall of the Western Roman Empire. It was largely deprived of its wealth and material resources, but it had managed to retain its prestige. Christianity was still the religion in most of post-Roman Europe, which was now essentially governed by pagan kings.

From the sixth century, early popes of the Roman Church tried to leverage this situation by offering Christianity to barbarian kings as a source of legitimacy and a way of identifying with the old power of the empire. This resonated deeply with the people. One by one, barbarian kings accepted this opportunity, converting to Christianity. The conversion of a leader would prompt his subjects to also convert, resulting in a ripple effect that continued in Western Europe for about two centuries until most barbarian kingdoms were, at least in name, Christian.

Of course, it would take generations before the old pagan ways of life would be abandoned and a Christian society characteristic of the Middle Ages would become firmly established. Nevertheless, by the late seventh century, most of the old Western Roman Empire in Europe, including Italia, Gaul, Iberia, and Britannia, was under the control of Christian rulers. The Roman Church slowly became as important as it had been during the late Roman Empire. This became even more pronounced with the reign of Charlemagne.

Again, it is in Venerable Bede's *Ecclesiastical History of the English People* that we find the story of the conversion of the Anglo-Saxons. Even though he provides a rather simplistic account of the conversion, historians consider the general outline of his story correct.

The first Anglo-Saxon king to convert was King Ethelbert of Kent, sometime in the late sixth century. He had married a Merovingian Frankish princess, Bertha, daughter of Charibert I, who was a Christian. At the time, Canterbury was a prominent center in the Kingdom of Kent. It seems that after the arrival of Bertha, King Ethelbert allowed a Frankish bishop to restore an old chapel there. This points to King Ethelbert's already tolerant attitude toward freedom of worship.

It is possible that Ethelbert and his court requested that the pope send a Christian mission to their domains. At the time, the Roman Church was headed by Pope Gregory I, who became known as Gregory the Great for his efforts and very successful papacy. Pope Gregory endorsed many missionary activities early on, to the extent that the early Roman Church largely owed its renewed prevalence in post-Roman

Europe to him.

Obvious political circumstances would have made the Gregorian mission to the Anglo-Saxons, and especially to the court of King Ethelbert, a logical decision. First, Gregory wrote extensively to Frankish kings to aid the mission by sending monks and priests from their domains to accompany Augustine, a monk from Rome whom Gregory had chosen to lead the mission in 595. By involving the Franks, Gregory knew Ethelbert would be more inclined to receive it positively. (His wife was of Frankish origin and the Franks exerted great influence over Kent both economically and culturally.) Besides, Ethelbert had already allowed Bertha and a Frankish chaplain to practice Christianity in Canterbury.

Most importantly, the conversion of Kent would have been a big step toward the conversion of other Anglo-Saxon kingdoms, as at the time Kent was the most prominent of them. In any case, after departing Rome and suffering a series of initial setbacks, the Gregorian mission landed in Kent in 597.

Bede's account of the conversion of the Anglo-Saxons is very optimistic and biased. His depiction of the events that followed the conversion of Ethelbert, which most likely took place in 597, describes an eager population and a chain reaction of conversion of other kingdoms that only ended in the 660s. Though Bede equates the conversion of a leader to the conversion of the rest of his subjects, this notion is only partially true even when applied to societies with a strong relationship between the leader and his subjects, such as the Anglo-Saxons.

Ethelbert's conversion was not solely motivated by religious reasons; clear political motivations were behind this move. It also appears that Ethelbert did not actively force his subjects to convert and only loosely promoted Christianity. Though some members of his court followed through and converted, it is unlikely that most of the Anglo-Saxon population accepted Christianity in the next few years. Pope Gregory's letter to the Church in Alexandria, dating to 598, mentions that ten thousand Anglo-Saxons had been converted. Also, by the year 601, the mission that had been firmly established at Canterbury reported back to Rome, asking for additional resources to expand Christianity outside of Kent. This suggests that the missionaries might have faced difficulties.

The Christianization of Anglo-Saxon England took generations. King Caedwalla of Wessex, for example, referred to as the last pagan Anglo-Saxon king, did not convert until 688, and his baptism took place in Rome. Moreover, active campaigns against paganism were likely directed by the kings only in the late seventh century.

Before that, it appears that pagan and Christian kings alternated in Anglo-Saxon kingdoms. A king would convert to Christianity, but his successor would revert to paganism, halting the spread of the religion. For example, after the death of Saberht of Essex, a nephew of Ethelbert who was baptized in the latter's court in 604, his successors—Sexred and Sæwred —continued to promote paganism from 613 onward. Paganism would persist in Essex until the middle of the seventh century before King Sigebehrt was convinced by King Oswiu of Northumbria to adopt Christianity in 653.

Overall, this might have been the reason that communication between the Church in Britain and the papacy also declined between the late 620s and the late 650s. The situation was chaotic, with individual kings trying to assert their dominance over the Christian bishops who would gain prominence during the reigns of previous kings, and so on. External reasons, like relations with the Christian Franks, might have also influenced the maneuverings of the Anglo-Saxons throughout the seventh century.

Complications also came from the type of Christianity adopted by the Anglo-Saxon rulers and their subjects, as the Gregorian mission to Kent does not appear to be the only Christian influence, especially in the eastern and northern Anglo-Saxon domains. Wessex, Northumbria, and Mercia were all influenced by Christian missionaries coming from Scotland and Ireland. It was not until the Synod of Whitby in 664 that the rulers of the heptarchy came together to erase the differences in their respective Christian worship.

If we consider the fact that Roman Britons had practiced Christianity well before the Gregorian mission, it is also likely that many people who appeared to have been Christian to Bede, Augustine, and other early Christian figures were Britons and not Anglo-Saxons.

Thus, in the 660s, the papacy appointed Greek Theodore as the head of the Church in Canterbury to unify the differences between Scottish, British, and Anglo-Saxon Christianity that had been promoted by the papal missionaries. The Church in Anglo-Saxon England clearly needed to be reorganized. Theodore's efforts, which included actions like reorganizing the existing English dioceses and redistributing resources to different bishoprics, culminated in the clarification of doctrine at the Synod of Whitby, held in the Kingdom of Northumbria. As he wrote the *Ecclesiastic History* in 731, Bede regarded Theodore's reforms as essentially the golden era of Anglo-Saxon Christianity.

Anglo-Saxon rulers, just like other barbarian kings in Europe after the fall of Rome, were attracted to Christianity to exploit the political positives that it brought. Besides being a way to identify with the great Romans as an essential element of the *Romanitas*, or "Romanness," Christianity also brought a mysticism that reconfirmed the powers of the kings in different aspects.

From early on, Christianity in Anglo-Saxon England helped restructure religious life around the royal family and the king and away from the powerful pagan priests. It managed to achieve this effect in an entirely aesthetic manner, as well. Kingship became grander, increasingly resembling the lavishness of the old Roman emperors who were exalted during their lifetimes—the best of whom were perceived to possess qualities that put them above others in the social hierarchy. The royal regalia of Anglo-Saxon kings became more precious and pronounced, sometimes even excessive, made from imported luxurious materials such as silk and containing more and more jewelry. Whereas before they had been fellow tribal chieftains who had risen to prominence, the kings were now distinguished by their majestic nature.

Though it would be a while before Anglo-Saxon society would accept the idea that kingship was divinely ordained, the adoption of Christianity was certainly a calculated step toward consolidating the power of the Anglo-Saxon kings, who needed to be perceived as "kings." Christianity brought officials that would be very useful in this endeavor. Clergymen were literate and therefore knowledgeable, not only about religious matters but also about history, society, culture, and laws. Forging close relations with the Christian clergy thus meant forging close relations with people who could be of great use in the courts. This relationship thus became intertwined early on and had practical effects.

As Anglo-Saxons converted in increasing numbers and as Christianity became more entrenched in society, maintaining patronage over the clergy emerged as an expensive endeavor, one that only the richest of the nobility could sustain. Despite its costs, which included granting hides of land and numerous resources to the Church, the benefits of patronage were immense for the rulers. Kings who appointed bishops loyal to them were now essentially in charge of the territories under these respective bishoprics or dioceses. Appointment of loyal bishops in what would otherwise be considered "foreign" lands was, in fact, one of the ways kings increased their influence over their rivals. Over time, the ability to appoint religious officials to oversee territories became synonymous with kingship. As a result, lesser kingdoms, such as the Hwicce, were completely absorbed by larger kingdoms.

Overall, Christianity acted as a facilitator in governance and an accelerator of political cohesion in an unstable environment. The Anglo-Saxon rulers' adoption of Christianity was a conscious effort to reinvent and elevate early kingship to a new level.

By the middle of the eighth century, paganism had essentially been eliminated as a prevalent social and cultural force in the Anglo-Saxon kingdoms. The Anglo-Saxon Church, at first divided according to the political influences of separate leaders, now adhered to the principles and doctrines promoted by the Roman Church and administered by two archbishops: of Canterbury, since 669, and of York, since 735.

The result was a completely different political landscape, with fewer and larger kingdoms of the heptarchy having eliminated the smaller distinctions based on tribal lineage. In addition to the homogeneity introduced by Christianity, a common "English" language had also fully developed from the old dialects of the Angles, Saxons, and Jutes, providing the basis for a shared sense of identity. Still, despite this, the political rivalries between the largest kingdoms were all but over.

Chapter Four – Mercian Supremacy

In this chapter, we will look at the period of Anglo-Saxon history that follows their Christianization. This era, lasting from the early eighth to the middle of the ninth century, is often differentiated as the time of "Mercian Supremacy"—a term coined in the early twentieth century. This is because the Kingdom of Mercia emerged as the most dominant kingdom in Britain for about a century and a half. Mercia's supremacy, spearheaded by the succession of its powerful kings Ethelbald and Offa, was manifested in the political, economic, and cultural domination of its neighbors. When we consider the factors that made Mercia the most powerful kingdom of the Anglo-Saxons in the eighth century, it is important to think about how close Mercia came to politically unifying Anglo-Saxon England. The developments in this period would lay further foundations for the notion of a united kingdom of England.

Rise of Mercia

An obvious peculiarity to note when discussing Mercian dominance throughout the eighth century is the lack of written documents produced in Mercia. In fact, most of what we know of the reigns of kings Æthelbald (Ethelbald) and Offa are from sources written in other kingdoms—for example, the works of a Benedictine monk named Boniface, who was from Wessex. Mercian rulers seem to only have commissioned charters. Later rulers, like Alfred the Great of Wessex, refer to the law codes produced in this period in Mercia, though there is a lack of archeological and textual evidence to confirm this.

Even though we know that Mercia was the strongest political and economic force in Britain at this time, the lack of documents suggests that the structural organization of Mercian power was very different from other dominant kingdoms of the time. Additionally, any such material could have easily been destroyed later, especially during the Viking invasions, which hit Mercia especially hard.

However, there is no reason to suspect that foreign chronicles had an active agenda against the Mercian kings or that their writings had an inherent bias. Still, their perspectives, especially when classifying the rulers' decisions, would have starkly differed from the accounts of those who operated closer to the royal courts of Mercia in the eighth century.

When we talk about the domination of Mercia throughout the eighth century, we should not forget that the kingdom had also been relatively strong in the previous hundred years. Its rulers were overkings of smaller kingdoms of central England and sometimes dominated parts of the south. King Penda, for example, who reigned until his death in 655, repeatedly waged successful wars against the Northumbrians, East Anglians, and West Saxons. During his reign, Mercian control over the Midlands became firmly established, and his influence spilled over to his successors. At this time, the Mercians also asserted their power over the kingdom of Hwicce and even occupied southeastern parts of England, such as London and Surrey. Thus, by the late seventh century, it can be said that Mercia was already positioned to dominate its rivals, though not to the extent that it would later.

The nature of Mercian dominance in the eighth century, therefore, stems mostly from two factors. First was the Christianization of Anglo-Saxon domains, tied in with the strengthening of kingship. The second factor was the longevity of two of its consecutive rulers —Ethelbald and Offa. In fact, the two are among the longest-ruling kings in Anglo-Saxon history. In comparison, there were more than ten Northumbrian kings in the same period.

Thanks to the influence of Christian clergy and territorial advances that former Mercian kings had made before their reigns, Ethelbald and Offa built upon the foundations presented to them and made Mercia the supreme Anglo-Saxon kingdom in Britain. They utilized their vast resources to introduce better methods of exercising royal authority on a grander scale and thus came in touching distance of creating the first

"English" state—though this was most likely never their intention.

Ethelbald became king of the Mercians in 716, succeeding his cousin, Ceolred, to the throne. Ethelbald had been in exile during Ceolred's reign (perhaps by Ceolred himself) for unknown reasons. The story of his accession is recounted in the *Life of Saint Guthlac*, written by an author named Felix for King Ælfwald of East Anglia, who reigned from 713 to 749. The author mentions that the exiled Ethelbald was in contact with Guthlac, a former Mercian nobleman who had retired from public life and was living as a Hermit in Crowland, in modern-day Lincolnshire. Guthlac had prophesized about Ethelbald becoming king, though he died two years before his prophecy was fulfilled. Exactly how Ethelbald took over the throne of Mercia is unclear, but his contact with Guthlac and the mention of him in an East Anglian source suggest that he was a favored candidate.

Whatever the exact story behind Ethelbald's accession, he appears to have become the most powerful ruler south of the Humber River over the next fifteen years, especially after the death of the kings of Wessex and Kent in 725 and 726. The Ismere Diploma, a charter issued by Ethelbald in 736 that records a grant of land to one of his subjects, attributes the titles "King of the Mercians and the South English" and *Rex Britanniæ*, "King of Britain," to Ethelbald. Though "King of Britain" should be considered a typical exaggeration, the other title is consistent with the account in *Ecclesiastical History*, where Bede calls Ethelbald the "overking south of the Humber." It is unclear if "south English" refers to all the peoples south of the Humber or just those considered Angles (inhabitants of Mercia and East Anglia), but it signifies the powerful position Ethelbald enjoyed during this time.

By the middle 730s, the Kingdom of Mercia under Ethelbald controlled significant territories south of the Humber and had considerable influence over their political affairs. For example, Ethelbald appears as the overking of Hwicce, southwest of the Mercian heartlands, which was ruled by a local royal dynasty subject to Ethelbald's rule. Mercian charters of the time mention this relationship. Other documents contain information about religious lands further to the east, in the areas around London, being exempt from taxes, which suggests the extent of Ethelbald's power there.

The influence of Ethelbald's rule further south—in the Kingdom of Kent, for example—was less pronounced. It can only be inferred from the fact that the three successive archbishops of Canterbury in the middle of the eighth century were Mercian. Kentish kings of the time appear to have granted lands without Ethelbald's direct involvement, suggesting that the extent of his political influence there was limited to religious institutions.

Ethelbald was also the overlord of London, sponsoring the activities of the Church there, and it was during his reign that the city finally fell out of the political influence of the kings of Essex.

Ethelbald's relationships with the kings of Wessex and Northumbria appear to have been more complicated, perhaps due to the relative strength of these kingdoms compared to Kent, East Anglia, or Essex. There is evidence he campaigned against Wessex as early as 733 and again in 740 against the new King Cuthred. Three years later, however, Cuthred and Ethelbald waged a common offensive against the Britons of Wales, suggesting that either Cuthred was subordinated by Mercia or the Britons were simply a faction they saw as a common enemy.

Thus, Bede's account of Ethelbald's over-kingship of the "English south of the Humber" should not be taken as the manifestation of a true hegemon. Anglo-Saxon kingship, though profoundly transformed by the introduction to Christianity, was still in its early stages of development. Likewise, communication channels were simply not developed enough to make Ethelbald the clear authority in the eyes of the southern English.

Despite this, the influence he had—especially over the dominions of the Hwicce, East Anglia and Essex—was certainly more than that of previous rulers, making it worthy of highlighting, even by a writer from a rival Northumbrian court.

Ethelbald also campaigned against Northumbria on two occasions, in 737 and 740. Though his offensives gained him little influence north of the Humber, it highlights that he was trying to exploit the weakness of Northumbria while King Eadberht was away fighting the Picts in the north. Some have also suggested that Ethelbald allied with the Picts to undermine Northumbrian dominance north of his realm. Whatever the case, Mercian military and political dominance during the reign of Ethelbald was confined south of the Humber.

Ethelbald's rule was controversial, to say the least. There is contrasting evidence about the nature of his relationship with the Church or even his "unchristian" conduct. Boniface accused Ethelbald of not respecting the principle of monogamy and of being an adulterer, for example, in addition to his exploitative and harsh treatment of the religious clergy. The first of these accusations might be explained by the prevalence of pagan or pre-Christian tendencies among Anglo-Saxon rulers, whose moral compass might not have been fully fixed to the new standards. His alleged harsh treatment of monks and bishops, on the other hand, might indicate that he viewed his influence over religious affairs as a political advantage.

His unpopularity is also supported by his cause of death in 757— murder. The Mercian king was murdered treacherously for unclear reasons. The fact that he was briefly succeeded by a nobleman named Beornred suggests a possible conspiracy, especially since Beornred's rule was cut short by Offa, who defeated the contender either in the same year or the following.

King Offa of the Mercians

Offa's reign, which lasted for thirty-nine years, is only similar to his predecessor Ethelbald's in the territorial extent of his power. His rule was concentrated in the Mercian Midlands and included London, which had emerged as a significant trading hub for early medieval merchants. Offa exerted more direct control over his subjects in Hwicce and Essex, often placing Mercian nobles in positions of power in these kingdoms and contributing to their political decline.

Unlike Ethelbald, he perceived himself simply as "King of the Mercians" and did not adopt superlative titles that claimed over-kingship of other kingdoms. The official charters he issued never attribute another title to him, unlike Ethelbald's. This might suggest that in his day, Mercian Supremacy was already seen as something normal and the territories he controlled were viewed as an enlarged Mercian kingdom, not a combination of smaller realms. Thus, there is no evidence that he intended to unify a nation of Anglo-Saxon or English people. Instead, he seems to have been motivated primarily by the pragmatic political goals of expanding power.

Much like Ethelbald, he confined the extent of his ambitions to the territories south of the Humber and did not pursue significant military gains in Northumbria. However, the fact that his daughter was married off to King Æthelred of Northumbria suggests he was not completely uninvolved.

King Offa of Mercia on a silver penny.
https://commons.wikimedia.org/wiki/File:Offa,_King_of_Mercia,_silver_penny;_(obverse).png

Where Offa and Ethelbald significantly differ is their perception of Christian kingship and the perception of their status through other actions.

Offa maintained regular correspondence with Charlemagne of the Carolingian Empire. However, his relationship with the Frankish Carolingian ruler was complicated, as evidenced by the letters they exchanged. Offa was indeed the most powerful king in Britain at the time, much respected by his contemporaries, including his rivals. However, in his correspondence with Charlemagne, he appears overly ambitious, and his ambitions are checked by the Carolingian emperor, who clearly did not view him as an equal.

Charlemagne was, for example, insulted when Offa asked for his daughter Bertha to be married to Offa's son Ecgfrith. Offa's request was a reciprocal proposition, as Charlemagne's court had requested for Offa's daughter to marry Charles, the son of the emperor. Insulted, Charlemagne issued a trade embargo on Mercian merchants in his lands. Offa reciprocated with an embargo on Frankish merchants trading on Mercian soil. Despite this, the two rulers maintained their relationship, lifting the trade embargoes by the late eighth century. Charlemagne even sent gifts to the Mercian king. At the very least, Charlemagne saw Offa as a respectable figure and a potential ally, whereas Offa was influenced by Charlemagne's grandeur and status.

Frankish influence on Mercia during the reign of Offa can be clearly observed in certain aspects. In the history of Medieval Europe, Christian kingship became the most prominent form during Charlemagne's reign. Charlemagne maintained very close relations with the papacy and pushed his image as a Christian monarch of Europe in the pattern of the old Roman emperors—manifested by his crowning as emperor in 800 by Pope Leo III. From his reign onward, the connection between royal authority and Christianity became more important throughout Europe. And Offa's Mercia was by no means an exception.

Offa began to emulate some of the royal practices of Charlemagne's court. For example, in 787, he anointed his son, Ecgfrith, as his co-ruler and intended successor, something that was done by Charlemagne and previous Frankish kings. Ecgfrith's anointing was carried out by a Christian bishop, essentially making him a legitimate successor and amplifying the relationship between the Church and royal authority. The assertion of kingship and transmission of power was thus made into a sacred ritual, resembling a Christian rite. Furthermore, Offa welcomed continental bishops into his court and promoted their missionary activities throughout his realm. The missionaries held a religious council after being received at Canterbury, which was attended by King Offa.

Offa was also strictly monogamous, something that constituted a conscious break from his pagan or Germanic identity. In fact, the image of his wife Cynethryth as the queen of the kingdom was also very prominent in eighth-century Mercia. In the official charters, she is mentioned as the "Queen of the Mercians," and archeological evidence includes coins minted in her name. All this suggests a close interrelation between the status of the queen and her public image as such. It was yet another manifestation of Christian kingship: the king had one wife who was the queen of the kingdom and supported the king by being involved in the affairs of the court. Monogamy provided legitimacy, a sense of civility and Christianity, and a sustainable lifestyle for Offa—something to be emulated by future Anglo-Saxon monarchs.

King Offa died in 796 from natural causes. Ironically, though he had tried to guarantee a safe and fruitful reign for his son Ecgfrith by involving him in court affairs during his lifetime, Ecgfrith's reign lasted for only a few months. He also died unexpectedly in December of 796. Alcuin of York, a contemporary teacher from Northumbria and a disciple of Archbishop Ecbert, mentions in his letters that King Offa had dedicated his life to preparing Ecgfrith to be the next king, only for God to decide his heir's fate.

Cenwulf, a cousin of Ecgfrith from another branch of the family, became king in late 796, inheriting a large kingdom in dire need of a strong ruler to maintain stability. As time would tell, Cenwulf was such a leader, ruling until 821 and retaining Mercia's influence as the largest and most powerful of the Anglo-Saxon kingdoms. During his reign, the role of the king of Essex diminished. In the charters issued by Cenwulf, the king of Essex eventually appears as an ealdorman—a former local king who had become a vassal of a greater king (eventually, the word *earl* would come to replace *ealdorman*).

In addition to Essex, Cenwulf reasserted Mercian rulership over East Anglia and Kent, which had most likely broken free from Mercian control after the unexpected succession of 796. King Eadberht III had gained influence in Kent, driving out the Mercian-appointed Archbishop of Æthelhard and sacking Canterbury. Interestingly, when declaring war on Kent, Cenwulf sought a judgment from Pope Leo III, who had excommunicated Eadberht, to show that his war on Kent was justifiable and Christian.

Despite Cenwulf's early victories, however, the early ninth century would prove difficult. The main problem Cenwulf had to deal with was the succession of Wessex. The heir, Ecgberht, who had been forced into exile by King Offa, returned to Wessex and defied Mercian domination. To reimpose his authority, Cenwulf launched an invasion against Ecgberht but did not achieve his goals. Wessex retained its independence.

Most of the pressing political problems Mercia encountered during the period of its dominance were linked to having to constantly assert control over its subjects through military means. And, though Mercian was among the first of the Anglo-Saxon kingdoms to consistently militarily dominate its neighbors, it would struggle to keep its gains permanent.

A New Society

There is much more to the era of Mercian domination than successful military conquests and political power. In fact, it can be argued that if it were not for the development of these aspects, the advances made by kings Ethelbald and Offa would not have been sustainable. The period of Mercian Supremacy encompasses socio-economic and cultural transformations that shaped the appearance of Anglo-Saxon life in the eighth century and became its staple for the next centuries.

The main economic factor that drove Mercia's dominance in this period was the drastic development of a network of cities that engaged in trade, known as emporia, mostly located on the eastern coast of England. During the first half of the eighth century, the emporia of Anglo-Saxon England, including London, York, Southampton, and Ipswich, began to expand. Archeological evidence suggests that economic activity in these areas peaked during the eighth century, and this was tied to population growth.

Increasing numbers of arrivals in these cities expanded and modified their layout to accommodate new infrastructural, civilian, and military projects. New roads and bridges were constructed to connect new settlements in areas around London and York to the old city centers. This led to the establishment of new small-scale factories and an increase in trade with continental Europe, especially with northern France and the Low Countries, which were Christianized Frankish domains by the ninth century. Ipswich, a town in what had been East Anglia before its submission to Mercia, developed industries such as pottery making, widely known throughout the Anglo-Saxon realms for its great style and quality.

Historians debate about whether the growth of these cities was stimulated by the policies of Mercian rulers or whether the rulers were simply lucky to rule during an era of growth. However, it is unlikely that an expansion of this scale in such a short time could have persisted organically without the involvement of authoritative figures to provide resources.

Traces of the involvement of "state officials" in the emporia's economic affairs can be observed as early as the late seventh century in Kent. As seen in the royal charters, these individuals were tax or tariff collectors for the Crown. Most likely, these royal servants taxed those who used the roads or entered Anglo-Saxon ports from abroad, as was the practice in continental Europe at the time.

In fact, this practice was most likely adopted from the Franks: under Charlemagne, Frankish traders were protected by the Crown if they were disadvantaged or oppressed in foreign lands. The close relationship between Frankish and Anglo-Saxon merchants can be seen from the incident when Charlemagne and Offa decided to issue embargoes on goods sold by Mercian or Frankish merchants.

In addition to kings, the Church, including local churches and monasteries, may have also contributed to this growth, as they benefitted heavily from the increase in trade, local production, and access to new trade routes. Many such institutions were exempt from taxes or tariffs under Mercian rule in exchange for promoting trade and the exchange of goods on a local level. For instance, the Church needed certain imported goods to conduct its religious ceremonies and rites, like olive oil or wine, which could only be imported from the continent.

Monasteries, which were often secluded from urban areas until small settlements inevitably popped up around them, were linked with the emporia through a network of administrative-type buildings. Located in remote areas of the country along trade routes, these sites include archeological evidence in the form of numerous coins and different local or foreign goods. These production sites likely served as both repositories of goods and administrative centers that further monitored trade and regulated supply and demand between different areas.

The centers of the Anglo-Saxon urban economy were also well supported by a growing rural economy, made possible by advancements in agriculture beginning in the seventh century. Food and raw materials would be supplied to the emporia through the production sites of these rural settlements, which were otherwise outside of the network of the main Anglo-Saxon trade routes.

Among the agricultural advancements of the time was a shift from subsistence farming toward a more diversified farming output. Seventh-century farms began cultivating crops that were also more profitable and supplied the markets of the emporia with their products. This also led to more organized farmlands, with clear demarcations. Archeological evidence also suggests the abandonment of old settlements when the yield no longer satisfied the required levels due to the exhaustion of the land. Historians believe that a large-scale move from such lands to richer soils explains the otherwise unclear abandonment of old settlements like Mucking in Essex, which had been inhabited for several thousand years before. Such changes caused a noticeable increase in rural agricultural production.

Changes to the structure of the Anglo-Saxon economy were heavily tied to the social and cultural changes taking place on a large scale throughout the eighth century. These changes were caused by the Christianization of the Anglo-Saxons, whose rulers were at least nominally Christian by the late seventh century. As Mercia rose to power, Christianity became even more entrenched in Anglo-Saxon society. It was slowly transforming from a society that had been Christianized to a society that was Christian.

This was partially because Christianity tapped into the everyday lives of ordinary people. It regulated most aspects of life from early on due to its many ceremonies and rituals. Though the same can be said of the pagan belief system, which was also based on frequent rituals, Christianity allowed for much less variation from individual to individual. Paganism was comparably a very individualistic religion.

Anglo-Saxon Christianity in the Eighth Century

The growing prominence of Christianity resulted in the development of a very effective network of churches, monasteries, bishoprics, and dioceses throughout Anglo-Saxon realms. The Anglo-Saxon elite, comprised of power-hungry aristocrats, began to exploit these developments in different ways, believing it was possible to gain more power and wealth with the help of Christianity. Exerting influence on the Church put the elites in a powerful position to influence the people, who listened to the friars and bishops and saw them as their spiritual guides throughout life. The Church and the ruling class of the Anglo-Saxons thus began to develop a symbiotic relationship early on. From the late seventh century, various churches and monasteries, which had acquired lands from the nobility, were freed from burdens to increase their influence.

Respecting this complex, mutually beneficial relationship was important. This can be seen from the history of King Ethelbald, who, as monk Boniface writes, greatly exploited the monks in Mercia during his reign. In 749, Ethelbald appears to have fixed his relationship with the Church, exempting it from taxation everywhere throughout his kingdom and granting it the right to enjoy the products from the cultivated lands in its possession. Such privileges, in addition to the monasteries' increased role in domestic trade, accelerated the growth of the Church's power. By the dawn of the eighth century, the Church had been greatly enriched from all these advantages.

Monasteries founded throughout Anglo-Saxon realms from the late seventh century featured a diverse range of influences from neighboring cultures, including Irish, Frankish, and even Italian traditions. This resulted in a diverse range of monastic daily life patterns. Many monasteries were large and in remote areas secluded from the public, but this was not always the case.

In Old English, the word *minster* was used to refer to all Christian communities, disregarding their size or type of organization—a word with the same etymology as the Latin *monasterium*. Though the word was eventually replaced by the term "monastery," it was later used as a title for particular churches throughout England. Among the prominent churches that feature the Old English name are the famous Westminster Abbey in London and the York Minster in Yorkshire. Minsters were endowed with rights by special royal charters.

English minsters had several critics by the mid-eighth century. The Venerable Bede, for example, writing in a letter to Bishop Ecgberht of York in 734, passionately criticizes the practices of monks in Northumbrian monasteries. He mentions corrupt nobles who gained royal charters to establish monasteries but knew nothing of the monastic tradition or Christian ways of life. Bede says that these individuals did not actively pursue Christian lifestyles, breaking many sacred rules such as celibacy and using the privileges that came with the charters to enrich themselves and accumulate wealth that could be passed down to future generations.

Essentially, Bede's criticism lay in the belief that monastic life must be entirely ecclesiastical, practiced solely by the clergy and not pursued by secular figures such as the nobility. He felt that the socio-political elites of the Anglo-Saxon community were encroaching on ecclesiastical life with their influences and undermining its independence.

Bede was not alone in his criticism, as the monk Boniface made similar accusations in his 747 letter to Archbishop Cuthbert of Canterbury. In it, he suggested the archbishop introduce the same reforms to the Anglo-Saxon Church that had been introduced in the Frankish Church. One of the necessary reforms was for laymen to be stripped of control over monasteries, Boniface asserted. He also mentioned that changes should be made in the behavior and appearance of the clergy. For example, bishops should dress in more modest attire.

These criticisms would be addressed the same year at the Council of Clovesho—a special synod that had first convened five years earlier. The Council of 747 was attended by the clergy from the Archdiocese of Canterbury and King Ethelbald of Mercia. After much discussion and deliberation, the synod proclaimed a series of canons that must be observed in monasteries, addressing apparent shortcomings among the members of the clergy such as instances of debauchery and drunkenness or arrogance and luxurious lifestyles. The council also sought to introduce clearer boundaries for the involvement of laymen—most importantly, of Anglo-Saxon nobility—in the religious affairs of monasteries. The council suggested that local bishops investigate local monasteries under the control of wealthy aristocrats to solve the possible problems addressed by Bede and Boniface in their letters.

It appears the council aimed to better define the borders between secular and ecclesiastical life while not publicly condemning the aristocracy for exploiting Christianity for personal gain or issuing extreme punishments such as excommunication. As we can see from the council's proceedings, the Anglo-Saxon Church of the eighth century was certainly in a bittersweet rivalry with the Anglo-Saxon political elites. It recognized that the quick spread of Christianity was largely due to the Anglo-Saxon nobility's involvement, but it was also critical of the nobility for not upholding high standards of ecclesiastical life in the monasteries under their domains.

Criticism directed at the heavy involvement of secular leaders in religious institutions was rooted in truth. However, the Anglo-Saxon Church had its own problems with the constantly shifting political climate and the association of certain religious institutions with certain rulers. Kings Ethelbald, Offa, and Cenwulf would often provide patronage to monasteries and other religious institutions located in conquered territories. This would bring these institutions under the king's direct influence, serving their agenda when it came to, for example, spreading the political power of Mercians over their newly acquired subjects. Ninth-century Kentish monasteries, for example, though nominally under the control of the Archbishopric of Canterbury, were mechanisms for Mercian kings to gain firm political control. The clergy that operated in these institutions were by no means exclusively loyal to the Church, leading to the outbreak of many disputes.

Even though the nobility's involvement in religious affairs during the eighth century brought many problems and criticisms, it is difficult to deny the nobility's material contributions to the development of a unique intellectual and artistic culture. Contact with the Frankish Church was vital in this regard. During the reign of Charlemagne, the English clergy often visited the Frankish court. From there, they brought back different texts and encouraged scholarship in English monasteries.

Developments in intellectual and artistic fields went hand-in-hand for the Anglo-Saxon Church. Insular art, sometimes referred to as Hiberno-Saxon art, is an amazing combination of Anglo-Saxon and Celtic-Irish Christian elements, leading to a style of religious art that was far different from that on the continent. The influence of Irish Christianity is especially evident in Northumbria due to the kingdom's close ties with the Celtic people from Ireland and Scotland.

There are many examples of insular-style religious manuscripts produced in Anglo-Saxon kingdoms during this period. The *Lindisfarne Gospels*, made in Northumbria in the late seventh century, is a Gospel book that bears elaborate, lavish decorations and a distinct style. It features the portraits of the four evangelists and other decorations, such as those on the carpet pages before the beginning of each gospel. This and other manuscripts, such as the earliest surviving Gospel book, the *Book of Durrow*, and the 236-page *Lichfield Gospels*, clearly demonstrate the peak of artistic influences on Anglo-Saxon art in the late seventh to early eighth centuries. These influences persisted until about the tenth century when they were perhaps disrupted by the Viking invasions.

Folio from the Lindisfarne Gospels.
https://commons.wikimedia.org/wiki/File:LindisfarneFol27rIncipitMatt.jpg

The Hiberno-Saxon insular style is also prominent south of the Humber in the realms controlled by Mercia during the eighth century, even though Celtic Christianity had been less prominent in these areas in previous centuries. Here, however, alongside insular elements, Anglo-Saxon art adopts continental influences, drawing heavily from classical and Italian styles. These influences appear clearly in works such as the *Vespasian Psalter*, an illuminated psalter produced at Canterbury in the first half of the eighth century, or the *Stockholm Codex Aureus*, a Gospel book also produced at Canterbury that contains purple parchment decorations resembling old imperial style manuscripts. These books, alongside other works such as the *Book of Nunnaminster*, bear a distinct artistic style deemed "Tiberius style."

Illuminated books weren't the only type of art produced in Anglo-Saxon England during this period. In the eighth century, a unique style of sculpture developed on both sides of the Humber River. Archeological evidence has found a diverse array of such sculptures in Mercia, dated to the late eighth century, that feature a combination of Anglo-Saxon, insular, and classical artistic styles.

The relationship that developed between the Anglo-Saxon Church and the laity was complex and multifaceted. Since the life of a commoner was a Christian one, the Church had the authority and knowledge not only to give general instructions but also to carry out activities to meet the spiritual needs of the laity. Among these were the typical Christian activities of communion, confession, and baptism, for example, as well as other rites such as preaching on Sundays.

Monasteries or other religious institutions were often faced with a range of problems with providing such services to the laity. The most obvious one was that the liturgies were often conducted in Latin, which was unintelligible to most laypeople. Thus, most probably did not understand the meaning behind the passages of the Bible read aloud by the priests. This problem existed among members of the clergy, as well, as many priests in smaller or rural monasteries had simply memorized the Latin phrases of the Mass and could not reliably read or understand Latin. This was one of the problems mentioned during the Council of Clovesho in 747, where it was suggested that the Mass be spoken in Old English in some areas instead of Latin. However, this change was never implemented by the clergy. The council generally encouraged better contact between the laity and members of the clergy for the laypeople to be more actively and passionately involved in spiritual activities.

In conclusion, in addition to large-scale changes in the political climate of Anglo-Saxon England throughout the eighth century, profound social, economic, and cultural changes were also taking place. Mercian domination was supported by an increase in economic activity and a better reorganization of social structures that accelerated growth and interconnectivity. Increased political, economic, and cultural contacts with other societies, most prominently with the Franks under Charlemagne, resulted in the introduction of new influences in all aspects of life. For most of the century and a short period afterward, Mercian kings were greatly respected. They had dominated their rivals on a previously unseen scale. In addition to economic stability, their supremacy was also upheld thanks to their complex relationship with religious structures, which ultimately served as a means of further increasing royal influence in distant lands.

Culturally, Anglo-Saxon England during the era of Mercian Supremacy saw the entrenchment of Christianity as the undisputed major religion and socio-cultural force. The Church established itself as a more respectable and powerful institution, gaining more structure and stability during the reign of the Mercian kings. It also spearheaded the development of a unique Anglo-Saxon art style as it sought to combine influences from neighboring cultures into something wholly distinct.

The Mercian kings had not united all Anglo-Saxons into a single kingdom and did not appear to have intended to. Most of the time, they acted out of pragmatic material interests, but in so doing managed to achieve great power and exert great influence over their rivals. But, as new forces appeared in Anglo-Saxon England in the ninth century, the era of Mercian Supremacy swiftly came to an end.

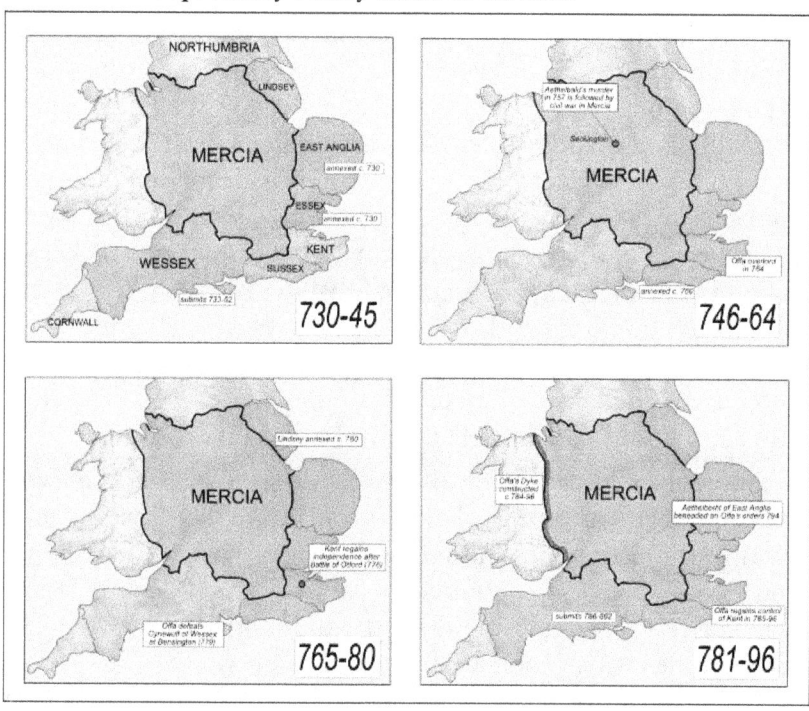

Illustration of Mercia's expansion of power.
Hel-hama, CC BY-SA 3.0 <https://creativecommons.org/licenses/by-sa/3.0>, via Wikimedia Commons; https://commons.wikimedia.org/wiki/File:Mercian_Supremacy_x_4.svg

Chapter Five – Anglo-Saxons and the Viking Age

In this chapter, we will look at the events of the ninth century that profoundly transformed the social, cultural, and political landscape of Anglo-Saxon England. This period marked the gradual decline of Mercian Supremacy in Britain as the most prominent Anglo-Saxon kingdom. In its stead, the Kingdom of Wessex rose, checking the former Mercian power before establishing supremacy over its rivals. More importantly, however, the ninth century saw the Anglo-Saxon kingdoms confronted with their biggest threat yet—the Vikings. Though the story of the Viking invasion of Britain has become widely known, the Vikings are much more than pragmatic and bloody military raids. The arrival of the Vikings marked a turning point for Anglo-Saxon kingdoms, forcing them to reconsider their differences and adopt new strategies to fight off a common enemy. This chapter will thus look at the history of the Anglo-Saxons during the Viking Age to uncover the challenges they would face hundreds of years after the first infamous Viking raid.

The Vikings

The Vikings would first come to raid the Anglo-Saxons in 793, landing at the northeastern settlement of Lindisfarne, then part of the Kingdom of Northumbria. There, they pillaged the monastery and decimated the locals. The violent, ruthless nature of the sudden attack on a religious institution by pagan foreigners caused a shock in the Anglo-Saxon realms and beyond. The Anglo-Saxons had been in contact with people from Scandinavia since migrating to Britain but had never before engaged in warfare with them.

Alcuin of York, a former Northumbrian scholar who had already joined Charlemagne's court when the raid in Lindisfarne took place, expressed in his letters the horror he had felt from what he deemed a barbaric attack that had desecrated Christianity. He sought to justify the destructive raid as a God-sent punishment for the wicked and unchristian way of life of many Northumbrians and warned that he feared the attack had not been the last one. Alcuin was right—the Vikings came back to Northumbria the next year and continued to frequent northern monasteries, plundering Tynemouth and Hartness by the end of the eighth century. Yet, Alcuin could never imagine the scale of the Viking invasion that was to come to England decades after the first raid at Lindisfarne. The Vikings had not yet become the greatest threat to the Anglo-Saxons.

Northumbria wasn't the only place where the Vikings would make their presence known in the period of about three hundred years known as the Viking Age. Scandinavian Norsemen raided, colonized, conquered, and traded with people across Europe. They established close relations with the Franks, who were becoming the most dominant force in Europe at the time, and reached the Atlantic coast of Iberia and raided some Mediterranean cities. Their ruthless attack on northern France eventually gained them recognition by the Frankish king, as well as a substantial piece of land called Normandy. They established a presence in the Faroes, eastern Ireland, and other smaller islands of the British Isles. Further west, they reached places nobody in Europe had even heard of, founding colonies in Iceland and Greenland and even journeying as far as North America and making landfall at Newfoundland.

Masters of seafaring, the Vikings would also utilize the vast network of major rivers in Eastern Europe to reach major wealthy civilizations of the Near East—the Byzantine Empire and the Muslim world of the Middle East—and travel through the domains of the Kievan Rus and the Black and the Caspian seas. The Vikings would be revered by these peoples for their brilliant military skill and tradesmanship, emerging as some of the most dominant and compelling actors in Europe until the eleventh century.

The image we have of the Vikings as ruthless, ale-consuming warriors with horned helmets comes from contemporary Christian sources that inevitably depict them as pagans and heathens and are appalled by their savagery. The Christian world—before the Vikings themselves would accept the religion—was certainly a victim of their warmongering for a long time, but it would be unfair to only mention the Vikings in this context. In fact, much Viking activity during the Viking Age was concerned with exploration, colonization, and trade, not just military conquest, piracy, and raiding.

The dramatic expansion of Viking influence from the late eighth century has been explained by a few factors. One possible explanation is their comparably tough living conditions in Scandinavia. A potential population boom during the early eighth century would have forced the Scandinavians to search for new areas to settle in as their land became incapable of meeting their increased demand for food. Their decision to begin raiding seems logical from this perspective.

Another explanation for the quick ushering in of the Viking Age credits technological breakthroughs as the main catalysts behind the Vikings going out to sea. Developments in shipbuilding techniques and improvements in navigation were crucial factors in the distinct Viking identity. New ship designs allowed them greater maneuverability, giving them the option to navigate through European rivers, as well as durability and speed.

In addition to these theories, the economic explanation also stands out. The economic recovery and growth of eighth-century Europe after the fall of Rome in 476 could have served as a motivation for Scandinavians to exploit new trade routes and wealthier cities in northern and western Europe. More expensive trade goods were circulating during this period, and the growing Anglo-Saxon, Frankish, Slavic, or even Muslim trading centers seemed like good targets for the Vikings. Scandinavia was first exposed to the trade routes in the northern and eastern parts of Europe, eventually reaching the richer cultures of the Mediterranean basin, such as the Byzantine Empire.

In addition to goods, traders and merchants from different states also exchanged information—a commodity that was just as useful in many cases. They brought news of the places they had visited, including stories about their wealth and political and military weaknesses, crises, or local conflicts. It is not unlikely that one motivation of the Vikings was to exploit these opportunities by launching raids in lands they considered chaotic or unstable, such as the realms of the Anglo-Saxons.

As we have already partially mentioned, the earliest attacks of the Vikings in Anglo-Saxon England were not directed at the richer trade centers, such as the emporia in London or Ipswich. Instead, the initial targets of Viking raids were poorly defended religious institutions, such as monasteries. In the previous chapter, we touched on the material wealth that was present in Christian churches and monasteries of the time, thanks to either patronage from the local elites or to the churches functioning as local centers of trade. In other words, they constituted prime targets that held decent wealth but were also relatively easy to plunder. Although contemporary Christian writers present Viking raids as targeted pagan attacks on Christianity, this was not a tangible motivation of the Vikings.

The End of Mercian Supremacy

In the previous chapter, we talked about the strength of the Anglo-Saxon Kingdom of Mercia during the eighth century. The reigns of Ethelbald and Offa made Mercia ambitious and powerful, but the prosperity of their time would gradually end as Mercia entered its period of decline in the early ninth century. Offa's successor, Cenwulf, can be considered the last great Mercian king, ruling until the year 821, but his rule faced many challenges early on. Imposing over-kingship on lesser kingdoms had always proven to have been a burdensome task for any monarch, but more problems began to arise in the early ninth century. As we mentioned, Cenwulf faced much opposition from the lesser kingdoms, most prominently from Wessex, which rebelled soon after the death of Offa and refused to submit to the Mercians. By the year 825, there were already clear signs of Mercia's declining political power in England.

All in all, the following developments in the Anglo-Saxon realms during the ninth century coincided with an increasing amount of Viking activity in England. The Vikings posed a significant threat to the Anglo-Saxons at a time when they were among their weakest—immediately as the Kingdom of Mercia was losing its control and influence.

The events of the ninth century are mentioned mostly in the *Anglo-Saxon Chronicle*, which presents Wessex's viewpoint on the developments that led to the decline of Mercia. The *Chronicle* mentions that the East Anglians approached Ecgberht of Wessex for help against the Mercians after the passing of Mercian King Ceolwulf—Cenwulf's brother—in 823. At this point, Mercia was plunged into a succession crisis. The armies of Ecgberht decisively defeated the Mercians at the Battle of Ellendon in 825, near the modern town of Swindon, forcing the kingdom to give up its hopes of over-kingship of East Anglia and Kent.

In fact, from 825 onward, Mercian invasions into these lesser kingdoms would no longer result in submission to Mercian rule. We know this from the coins minted in late 820s East Anglia, which bore the name of its local king instead of a Mercian one. Though Mercian kings continued to grant royal charters to some of the religious institutions in East Anglia in the next decades, the real extent of their power and influence was limited compared to a hundred years earlier.

Despite these shortcomings, the Kingdom of Mercia was a strong Anglo-Saxon kingdom during the middle of the ninth century. Certainly, the ambitions of Mercian kings never ceased, as seen in renewed invasions of Wales to extend Mercian influence there, as well as royal marriages with other Anglo-Saxon kingdoms, such as one between Mercian King Burgred and West Saxon princess Æthelswith in 853. Still, Mercia was only a shadow of its former self by this time.

Meanwhile, the Kingdom of Wessex was slowly assuming its position as the new potential power among the Anglo-Saxons. There, King Ecgberht founded a ruling dynasty in 802. With East Anglia's request to help against Mercia, Wessex became more concerned with spreading its influence in Anglo-Saxon realms, as it had primarily waged wars in the west against the Celts during the first two decades of the ninth century. The victory against the Mercians seemed to turn the tide in Wessex's favor.

King Ecgberht proved to be an ambitious ruler. Following his victory, he launched an offensive into Kent, deposing a Mercian-appointed sub-king, which gave him virtual control over southern Anglo-Saxon domains. Then, in 829, according to the *Anglo-Saxon Chronicle*, Ecgberht campaigned against the Mercian King Wiglaf, who was unrelated to the royal line of Mercian kings, and decisively defeated him.

The *Chronicle* mentions that a few years later the Northumbrians also submitted to the West Saxon king at Dore in modern-day Sheffield, granting King Ecgberht the title of *Bretwalda*—which roughly translates to "overking" of Britain, or "Britain-wide" ruler. This title only appears in the *Anglo-Saxon Chronicle* and most likely serves to glorify the achievements of King Ecgberht and his successful undermining of Mercian Supremacy during his reign. Though it is unlikely that Ecgberht was a Britain-wide ruler, the use of the title suggests that he nevertheless held considerable power by 830.

Ecgberht's over-kingship of Mercia and Northumbria was brief and not exactly profound. This is affirmed even though coins were minted in the name of King Ecgberht as "King of the Mercians." Wiglaf returned in 830 and reclaimed the Mercian throne, either forcefully or, more likely, through negotiation with Ecgberht. On the other hand, the Northumbrian King Eanred's submission to Ecgberht at Dore appears to have been voluntary in exchange for tribute—though this is not mentioned in the *Chronicle*. What we can reasonably infer is that Wessex would be overstretched if it tried to impose its dominance over such vast lands in the north as Mercia and especially Northumbria.

In comparison, the West Saxon over-kingship of Kent, Sussex, and Essex was much more expressed. These areas stayed under the influence of Wessex even as Viking raids intensified throughout the ninth century. They enjoyed a great deal of security, especially compared to Mercia and Northumbria, which took the brunt of the Viking invasion. Stable control of these areas was linked to another crucial factor in the succession of West Saxon kings after Ecgberht: the line of succession was direct, culminating in the accession of King Alfred the Great and, eventually, his grandson Æthelstan, who became the first King of the English in 927. The unbroken chain of succession is a testament to the extent of the strength of the Kingdom of Wessex compared to the more fragile Mercia.

It is interesting to examine other political and social factors that provided stability for the emerging Kingdom of Wessex, soon to become the most dominant of the Anglo-Saxon kingdoms. One of the main reasons for the success and longevity of West Saxon rule was the coherence of the kingdom's political and administrative structures and the distribution of royal offices. Importantly, the ealdormen in the Kingdom of Wessex were royally appointed officials who exercised authority in certain areas. Differently from Mercia, where divisions between administrative regions appear to have been less clear, the administrative divisions of Wessex were far more coherent. These units in the Kingdom of Wessex, be they shires or other divisions, seemed to have been introduced by the central government. They were centered on prominent urban areas rather than on the old, roughly defined dwelling areas of local peoples. For example, the region of Dorset, administered by a royally appointed ealdorman, was centered on the city of Dorchester.

The structural coherence of the West Saxon governance was supported by a wide range of sub-offices with clearly defined responsibilities organized in a strict hierarchical fashion. The royally appointed office of the minister is a prominent example. Though the *ministri* were present with limited responsibilities under Mercian rule, they appeared to be involved in a wide range of affairs during the era of Wessex. This can be seen from their frequent mentions in the royal charters. A typical West Saxon minister did not have the same range of power as modern-day ministers. Instead, these individuals held different positions, ranging from managing royal estates to being stewards or simple cupbearers for the king. Despite this, they were very close to the king, something that was naturally considered prestigious. Someone distinguished as a minister in the eyes of the king would have had the opportunity to advance in the hierarchy of royal officials, perhaps even rising to the rank of an ealdorman and holding considerable power.

Anglo-Saxon Society in the Ninth Century

The decline of Mercian power was also accelerated by the changing socio-economic conditions of the Anglo-Saxon kingdoms throughout the ninth century. Archeological evidence suggests significant economic developments south and north of the Humber.

In Northumbria, for example, there is evidence that the currency was progressively debased, perhaps a conscious choice by the Northumbrian kings to affect the kingdom's economy. There are increasingly more base-metal Northumbrian coins found from the middle of the ninth century. This suggests the decision was directed toward making it easier to complete simple transactions between commoners. Northumbrian coins from this period have been found in East Anglia, for example, suggesting that locals preferred to use such coins for everyday transactions.

In other Anglo-Saxon kingdoms, however, a general economic decline was marked by a drastic reduction in the volume of circulating currency. And though the evidence we have of coin usage in this period is insufficient to explain the economic decline, the changing level of coins in circulation does suggest a shift in the nature of their usage.

Archeological evidence also reveals a general decline in the social and economic activities in the most prominent Anglo-Saxon emporia. It appears that few new buildings were constructed in the most active economic areas of these cities from the late eighth century onward, suggesting a halt in economic growth. There is also evidence of less maintenance of these centers, resulting in the worsening condition of infrastructure.

Curiously, the ninth-century emporia appear to have decreased their manufacturing in industries such as textile-making, weapons crafting, pottery-making, and metalworking. Some trading sites, such as Lundenwic in modern-day London, which had been a community with a bustling social and economic life during the era of Mercian Supremacy, entered a period of decline in the late eighth century.

In addition to a smaller scale of activities, this decline was marked by the emporia shrinking in size. The diminishing power of the emporia also adversely affected other types of settlements that had been actively involved in the economic system of Anglo-Saxon kingdoms about a century earlier. Many smaller in-land trading posts and productive repositories that connected rural areas and urban centers either stagnated or were fully abandoned.

The existence of an external threat is one possible explanation for this shift in the socio-economic activity of ninth-century Anglo-Saxon emporia. Perhaps, the increased Viking activity in this period forced the inhabitants of these wealthy sites to become more conservative, hold onto their goods, or even entirely relocate. There is evidence of Viking activity in the southern Anglo-Saxon realms. The *Chronicle* describes the 842 Viking attack on London, for example, as very brutal, and London was targeted many times by the invaders in the middle of the ninth century.

This hypothesis can also be supported by the discovery of a ditch constructed in northern Lundenwic during this time. It is possible that the ditch was a defensive structure to keep the invaders in check. The increased presence of the Vikings in this period might have hindered the arrival of foreign merchants, who were afraid of Viking piracy and did not dare to cross the English Channel. Royal charters dating back to the later years of King Offa's reign mention the need to protect the waters of Kent and Sussex, for example, and even Charlemagne had decided to build a fleet to keep the northern shores of his vast empire safe from piracy. Thus, we know that external threat had existed for quite some time.

However, this explanation is only partial, as it appears that the decline of the emporia from their once-great status had already begun by the time the Vikings began to increasingly visit the Anglo-Saxon shores. There were most likely other reasons, as well. A change in environmental conditions is another factor that could have forced the inhabitants of productive sites to relocate to other centers, for example. There is also evidence of new settlements becoming magnets of urban growth in the later ninth and early tenth centuries. These settlements could have evolved as economic rivals to the emporia, which were so interconnected and dependent on each other that one's decline could have accelerated the decline of the others.

Despite this general trend of decline, however, some urban sites continued to flourish during the ninth century. This is most notable in Canterbury, an important British center since Roman times and both the royal seat and the archbishopric see since the early seventh century. Archeological evidence and royal charters reveal the intricate urban design of the walled city, with a high level of infrastructural maintenance and even local regulations for constructing new buildings—they needed to be a certain distance apart to allow for rainwater to effectively disperse. Canterbury was a densely populated city in this period, containing multiple burgages—plots of land rented out by the nobility or the king. Thus, the inhabitants of Canterbury enjoyed some of the highest quality properties of all the Anglo-Saxon urban areas.

The city also had a bustling life full of public areas such as marketplaces, as well as fraternities and guilds, each having a different purpose and organizational structure. Some of these guilds were concerned with maintaining public properties and the image of the city, while others focused on serving specific parts of the city's population, such as merchants or laborers. The city's mints were also among the most active throughout the Anglo-Saxon kingdoms, and a high volume of silver and gold coins suggests the increased wealth of Canterbury. All in all, when we consider the demise of emporia during this period, the economic might of Canterbury appears much more imposing.

Important developments were also taking place in the Church. The Church had accrued much material wealth thanks to donations from its early patrons and the social conditions that had allowed the religious institutions to prosper, at least economically. By the late ninth century, however, the Anglo-Saxon Church appears to have entered a crisis of learning, marked by a decrease in intellectual activity and ability. This constitutes the second characteristic of post-Mercian Anglo-Saxon society.

Life of King Alfred, produced by a Welsh biographer of the later West Saxon king, describes that the intellectual tradition that guaranteed the pursuit of knowledge had disappeared by the time Alfred became king. Latin had become a language that even the clergy themselves could not properly understand, let alone freely speak and translate into vernacular English. The knowledge of this fact was widespread, and the disrepute of the Anglo-Saxon Church was even alluded to by foreign bishops, who criticized the lack of important aspects of Church life such as regular synods, among other shortcomings.

In short, contemporary commentators allude to the fact that despite the existence of many wealthy religious institutions, they rarely followed a strict, disciplined Christian monastic life. Archeological evidence supports written sources—only a handful of manuscripts produced in the middle of the ninth century have been discovered. In the royal and legal charters, historians have identified the worsening quality of the Latin language and script. There is evidence of lessened activities in the scriptoriums of different monasteries, including in Christ Church at Canterbury.

In addition, an increasing number of royal documents produced in vernacular also suggest the gradual replacement of Latin with Old English. This is interesting considering the boom of social and economic activities in Canterbury. Again, the decline of Latin in Canterbury during the mid to late ninth century can be explained by the increasing Viking threat, which had forced many people to seek refuge inside the well-fortified walled city. This urban growth may have dramatically increased the prominence of Old English and caused a reciprocal decline in the use of Latin.

The situation might have been less severe in the western Anglo-Saxon domains, such as Wessex or the West Midlands of Mercia, where the tradition for learning and mastery of Latin maintained high standards during the middle of the ninth century. This is perhaps thanks to the continental influences present in these areas. For example, King Æthelwulf of Wessex had a foreign scribe in his court from Frankia, and the documents produced during his reign show a high-level mastery of Latin. Still, the situation was sufficiently bad enough that King Alfred envisioned a revival of learning and monasticism in his kingdom when he became king.

The Great Heathen Army

The Anglo-Saxon Chronicle does not mention that Viking attacks on Anglo-Saxon realms occurred from the very late eighth century to the middle of the ninth century. In fact, the *Chronicle* says nothing of Viking activity between 795 (two years after the attack on Lindisfarne) and 835, the date of its account of the Viking raid on Sheppey in southern England. For the next decade and a half, Viking raids were generally smaller, containing a force of thirty to forty ships each, at best. The *Chronicle* records battles throughout the 830s and 840s at Southampton, Hingston Down, and the River Parret, for example, providing few new details about the Vikings or the battles themselves.

It is in the invasion of 851 when the Vikings are described as having a considerably larger force of about 350 ships. This invasion, directed at Canterbury and London, seems to be the largest-recorded single Viking raid, and its scale can be confirmed by descriptions of Viking attacks in other contemporary sources. The Franks, for example, whose shores were just as exposed to Viking activity, recorded in the 840s that Viking raids contained hundreds of ships.

The nature of Viking activity appears to have changed around this time, as well. After their attack in 851, the Vikings did not go home for winter and instead stayed at Thanet, terrorizing the local population for a few months before deciding to set sail. Written sources claim that other Viking bands had acted similarly in Ireland, where the Vikings had emerged as frequent visitors around the same time.

Despite the increasing scale of Viking attacks year after year, the Anglo-Saxons resisted the foreigners with great success. The *Chronicle* (which we should remember is a source compiled in a West Saxon court) records that the kings of Wessex defeated the invaders on multiple occasions. For instance, King Æthelwulf of Wessex repelled the 851 invasion, accompanied by his son, Æthelbald.

It appears that the Vikings would strike a coastal area of England and proceed to overwhelm the local defenses for a time, but the response from Anglo-Saxon armies would be timely, eventually forcing the Vikings to retreat. We can infer from the way the *Chronicle* speaks of the

Vikings during the first half of the ninth century that it saw them as a recurring threat that could nevertheless be contained.

A new era of Viking invasions began in 865 with the arrival of what the *Anglo-Saxon Chronicle* calls the "Great Heathen Army," an army composed of a confederation of Danish, Swedish, and Norwegian Vikings. Though the exact size of this army is unclear, it probably contained no more than a few thousand raiders, most of them experienced warriors.

The Great Heathen Army landed in East Anglia, overrunning defenses and rampaging northward through the Anglo-Saxon countryside, reaching York by 866. To the horror of the Anglo-Saxons, the army was later reinforced by another force, dramatically increasing the danger they posed to the locals.

What differentiated the Great Heathen Army from previous Viking raids was that it intended from the very beginning to conquer and occupy the Anglo-Saxon lands instead of simply pillaging and raiding. Such clearly defined goals made cooperation among different Viking groups within the army possible. On the whole, it was a common practice for different Viking warbands to come together for raids, split the booty, and separate after the end of their attacks. In fact, achieving a force of this size, one worthy of being deemed "great," certainly suggests that despite the different Viking groups within the army, it was still very efficient and successful.

It is also unclear who exactly was in charge of the Great Heathen Army. According to legend, it was led by the three sons of the legendary Viking Ragnar Lodbrok, one of the most prominent Viking leaders of the Viking Age until that point. The legend tells that Ragnar's sons—Ivar the Boneless, Halfdan Ragnarsson, and Ubba—had joined their forces to avenge the death of their father at the hands of King Ælla of Northumbria, who had captured and executed Ragnar during a previous raid into his territory. The Nordic sources that mention the invasion also depict Ragnar as a half-mythical figure and a pioneer of Viking expansion and exploration, so they should not be considered historically accurate. Nevertheless, the fact that the Great Heathen Army was comprised of prominent Viking figures each leading their bands serves to emphasize its unique nature.

Having landed in East Anglia, the Vikings proceeded to make peace with the locals, who gave the invaders supplies and horses as made their way north toward York. The *Chronicle* mentions that the Kingdom of Northumbria was a prime target for the Vikings because of the political chaos of its succession crisis. At the time, the crown was contested between King Ælla and his brother Osberht. When we also consider the Nordic sources' statement that Ragnar's sons had wished to avenge the death of their father, it is clear the Vikings planned to attack Northumbria from the beginning and would have known of the difficulties the kingdom was facing.

By late 866, the Vikings had decisively defeated the Northumbrians, killing both Ælla and Osberht in battle and establishing themselves at York. For the next few months, they continued to ravage the Northumbrian countryside, imposing their rule on the local population and forcing them to pay *danegeld*—different kinds of tribute the locals would pay to the Vikings in exchange for peace, protection, or to dissuade their future attacks. Though the term was not used until later centuries, some Anglo-Saxons, including Northumbrians, had already been giving tribute to the Vikings by the time the Great Heathen Army landed in England.

After Northumbria, the next target for the Vikings was the Kingdom of Mercia, the largest Anglo-Saxon kingdom south of the Humber River, possessing thousands of acres of valuable farmland that was ripe for pillaging. The Vikings stayed at Nottingham for the winter of 867-868, where a combined Mercian-West Saxon army tried to check them. Despite the combined effort, however, the Vikings held off the Anglo-Saxons once again. It is likely that after the battle of Nottingham, the Vikings negotiated a peace agreement with the Mercians, probably in exchange for tribute, and left the kingdom alone for a few years.

The *Chronicle* remarks that the Great Heathen Army stayed in Northumbria throughout the winter but turned south and attacked East Anglia in 869. There, they resided in the town of Thetford, where King Edmund of East Anglia attacked them. The Vikings held out throughout the winter, emerging victorious in the battle against Edmund, killing the king.

East Anglia is the first Anglo-Saxon kingdom in the *Chronicle* that is said to have been entirely conquered by the Vikings one year after their initial attack in the winter of 869. The fact that East Anglia was small and one of the richest Anglo-Saxon realms at the time might have motivated the Vikings to take full control of it quickly. The *Chronicle* laments the perishing of the kingdom at the hands of the Vikings, a sentiment that seems cohesive with the public attitude at the time. Edmund would soon be venerated as a martyr, killed at the hands of the ruthless pagans.

Viking activity resumed in the second part of 871 when new bands of Vikings arrived from Scandinavia as reinforcements. They joined the main force at Northumbria and launched another attack on Mercia. This time, the Vikings targeted locations further south, reaching cities such as London and Lincolnshire by 872. Where possible, they tried to avoid confrontation with the Mercian army, instead choosing to overwinter in areas where they could sustain themselves solely by raiding.

This constant pillaging greatly affected the social and economic stability in Mercia. Mercian farmers and citizens lived in constant fear of the Vikings and could not properly access the farmlands in the countryside. The Vikings also posed a threat to some of the cultural centers of Mercia, such as when they targeted St. Wystan's Church at Repton, a site that held great material and spiritual importance for Mercian kings. St. Wystan's was where the royal Mercian mausoleum was located, and the strategic location of the site allowed the Vikings to exert firm control over the Mercian heartlands. The Vikings fortified their position at Repton, and archeological evidence suggests that they built defensive ditches and stayed in the town for a long time, even burying their dead there.

The *Chronicle* mentions that during this period, the Vikings forced King Burgred of Mercia into exile. The year 874 is considered the last year of his reign. Burgred traveled to Rome, probably on a pilgrimage, and died and was buried there. In his place, the Vikings installed a puppet king named Ceolwulf II, with whom they maintained a close relationship. The *Chronicle* says Ceolwulf was an "unwise" king who had sworn an "oath of loyalty" to the Vikings. Even though the Chronicle is a biased source, the dethronement of Burgred in favor of Ceolwulf indicates the influence the invaders had on the Mercian throne. Despite this, it is unlikely Ceolwulf was considered a fully illegitimate king, as he continued to issue royal charters for the five years he ruled, and the nobility and clergy who had also served under Burgred often acted as witnesses for his royal grants.

So, despite the Vikings installing a king they favored, it would be an exaggeration to say that they also put their own people in positions of power in the Mercian court. It seems more likely that Mercia was in a state of severe disarray and the local elites were unable or unwilling to resist the Vikings as long as they maintained their positions of power.

In his *Life of King Alfred*, Asser remarks that the Great Heathen Army split up sometime after their conquest of Mercia. One part of the army returned north to Northumbria and launched an invasion of the Picts in Scotland from there. The other part remained in the Anglo-Saxon realms, moving from place to place to maintain a strong hold on the conquered territories. It seems that the Vikings were content with having destabilized the Anglo-Saxons enough to make a united resistance very difficult; they still enjoyed the booty from constantly raiding the lands.

One kingdom the Vikings repeatedly tried to subdue was the Kingdom of Wessex, which, by 877, had done a relatively good job of keeping the Vikings at arm's length. The Great Heathen Army had raided West Saxon territories on several different occasions since its arrival in 865, but the responses from the kings of Wessex were swift.

Throughout the first years of the 870s, West Saxon kings Æthelred and Alfred were forced to make peace with the Vikings after suffering several defeats at their hands, first at Reading and Basing in January, and later at Wilton in April. These defeats forced the West Saxons to rethink their strategies, and King Alfred finally reached an agreement with the invaders in late 871. He also relocated further south to Winchester and proceeded to build a new force to drive the heathens out of England. Alfred was forced to make peace with the Vikings five years later when the invaders returned after having conquered Mercia. He was forced to give up more lands in the northern territories, and the Vikings essentially gained control of a large part of the northern, central, and eastern territories of Britain.

Alfred the Great

By 877, the Great Heathen Army had defeated the Anglo-Saxon kingdoms of East Anglia, Northumbria, and Mercia. The Vikings had established themselves comfortably in these lands, where any remnant of political leadership had dwindled throughout the 870s. The invaders had successfully installed a puppet king over the western half of Mercia, whereas they possessed the rich Midlands and the eastern territories, including London. Only the Kingdom of Wessex remained a valid Anglo-Saxon rival to the Vikings, and West Saxon kings had never managed to fight the Vikings on their terms.

As we mentioned earlier, a prominent Viking strategy was to quickly storm a poorly defended town, where they would organize their defenses. They would force the royal armies to approach them for negotiations and try to extort as much as possible. If the king refused to negotiate, the Vikings would either pillage the countryside until they had decimated the local population to force the hand of the king or simply relocate to another such town and repeat the process. Both kings of Wessex in this period, Æthelred and Alfred, had fallen victim to this Viking strategy. They had been unable to catch the Vikings off-guard, as the Vikings simply would not take a battle that would be unfavorable for them.

In 876, the part of the Viking army that was south of the Humber proceeded to thus take control of Wareham, in the southernmost part of Wessex, on the English Channel. There, they reached an agreement with Wessex about the exchange of hostages and maintenance of peace but quickly broke the agreement and relocated to Exeter. After this, the Vikings returned to Mercia, where, as we mentioned, they essentially divided the kingdom in two before returning to Wessex.

In January of 878, the Vikings launched a surprise attack on the royal stronghold of Chippenham. They overwhelmed the West Saxons here as well, forcing Alfred to flee with a small band of followers further north to Somerset, taking refuge in the remote village of Athelney. In the marshlands of Somerset, he set up his fortifications and planned to retaliate. From this remote area, Alfred began mounting a true resistance to the Viking invasion. The *Anglo-Saxon Chronicle* mentions that alone, against all odds, the king started to recruit local militia from Somerset, Wiltshire, and Hampshire during May of 878.

In late May of 878, King Alfred and his force were ready to strike. The king chose not to take the fight directly to Chippenham, where the Vikings, led by their warlord Guthrum, had fortified. Instead, as he gathered his recruits, Alfred drew the Vikings out and engaged in the decisive Battle of Edington with a few thousand men. The *Chronicle* does not mention the details of the battle, but it ended in a West Saxon victory, with the Vikings slaughtered on the battlefield. Alfred pursued the Vikings to the stronghold and laid siege, cutting off supply lines and forcing the Vikings to surrender two weeks later.

As part of the peace agreement, Guthrum converted to Christianity, and the Vikings swore an oath to leave West Saxon lands. Ultimately,

Guthrum and some of his men were baptized, and the Viking leader and King Alfred of Wessex agreed on a treaty that fixed the borders between the newly conquered Viking realms in central, northern, and eastern England and the areas under the leadership of Wessex in the south.

Alfred did not have to deal with the Vikings again until the 890s, when a different army raided the areas around Fulham. This time, however, Alfred quickly defeated the invaders and drove them out "by the grace of God." Thus, by the end of the ninth century, the great Viking invasion of Anglo-Saxon England was over.

King Alfred is not only one of the most central Anglo-Saxon figures but also among the most celebrated characters of early Medieval Europe. In popular culture, his image is that of the defeater of the Vikings and the "savior" of England. Alfred was, in fact, the Anglo-Saxon leader who dealt the decisive blow to the Great Heathen Army. Thanks to his efforts, the Vikings were driven back after more than a decade of rampaging through Anglo-Saxon lands. Still, it is perhaps misleading to think of Alfred as the person who defeated "the" Vikings, as they would launch many more invasions into Anglo-Saxon realms in later decades.

King Alfred was arguably also not the person who "saved" England. This is simply because there was no united "England" to save from a foreign invasion at the time. King Alfred's actions were primarily directed at defending his own Kingdom of Wessex, and he did not liberate the English lands that had been under Viking influence since the late ninth century. Even the final agreement he made with Guthrum stated that Alfred would mutually recognize Viking overlordship in these lands, which would eventually be known as the Danelaw ("the land with the Danish laws").

Still, King Alfred is not known as "the Great" for no reason. Though he did not decisively defeat the Vikings or "save" England, he was still the king who laid the foundations for creating a united kingdom out of the Anglo-Saxon realms. In fact, it can be argued that King Alfred's greatest contributions came after his victory at Edington—namely, the steps he took in nation-building that resulted in a united Kingdom of England a few generations later. Thus, it is just as crucial to examine the nature of Alfred's reign after the victory at Edington to truly see the magnificence that earned him a worthy title.

Map of Britain in 886.
https://commons.wikimedia.org/wiki/File:Britain_886.jpg

King Alfred is the Anglo-Saxon king about whom we know the most, by a wide margin. There were many high-quality documents produced during his reign or about his reign, including the *Life of King Alfred* and the *Anglo-Saxon Chronicle*, which provide us with valuable insights into his life.

And, though there is a lack of contemporary royal charters issued in Alfred's name, this is made up for by the fact that Alfred composed a law code for the first time among the Anglo-Saxons in over a hundred years. In addition, many other translated books were produced during Alfred's reign. These were composed by members of Alfred's court, religious figures under Alfred's patronage, or, in rare cases, Alfred himself. The king himself adapted several texts from Latin to Old English, such as St. Augustine's *Soliloquies*—a text that remains central to Christian philosophy today.

The fact that so many written texts linked directly to the king have survived signals different aspects of Alfred's reign. The first advantage is that it is possible to reconstruct Alfred's reign with great accuracy with the help of so many sources. This includes depictions of Alfred's personality and character, allowing us more insight into his life and the decisions that he made.

The survival of these texts also indicates that Alfred took great care of his public image as a Christian king who promoted learning and encouraged the production of new knowledge among his subjects. As we have said, this would have given him more authority in the eyes of the public. As Anglo-Saxon kings were being defeated by the Vikings, Alfred needed all the support he could get from his subjects by presenting himself as a strong king. His new law codex is a significant achievement in this regard, seeking to legitimize his rule through written text and force the profound transformation of West Saxon (or Anglo-Saxon society).

The production of such a large volume of texts also suggests that Alfred sought to be represented as the antithesis of the pagan Vikings who were the main adversary of his time. People would rather side with a king like Alfred who, unlike the Vikings, promoted learning and writing. Whatever the reasons, Alfred was certainly a monarch who cared about his public image and acted to reinforce it however he could.

Charlemagne had been the pioneer in such a transformation of the nature of kingship a hundred years earlier, and his successors had continued to assume and enforce this new understanding. The Frankish emperor may have been the main inspiration for King Alfred, especially when we consider that he needed to legitimize his rule.

Another reason King Alfred emerged as an example of what a king should be like came from the succession difficulties that had plagued the throne of Wessex since the middle of the ninth century. In fact, it was unlikely from the beginning that Alfred would become king, as he was the youngest of the four sons of King Æthelwulf. Wessex had been plunged into a succession crisis when Prince Æthelbald had assumed authority in 856 after his father, King Æthelwulf, had gone on a pilgrimage. As a result, the kingdom had been divided for many years, and all three of Alfred's brothers had emerged as kings. Wessex needed stability and a strong king, and Alfred could have been the key.

It is also very interesting to examine the early years of Alfred before he became king, as they can provide valuable insights into the formation of the future ruler's mind and way of life. Some historians have suggested that Alfred's upbringing might have played a big role in his religiosity and love for learning. As the youngest son, Alfred was likely expected to have a clerical career in the future, which was very common in medieval families where the oldest son would normally inherit the family possessions. Alfred's biography mentions that the king was interested in religious life from a very young age and always attended various ceremonies, such as daily and weekly sermons.

From a young age, the personality of the future king was already directed toward being engaged in activities that were normally neglected by the nobility. At their core, the Anglo-Saxon elites were descendants of old war chieftains and a society that valued violence and sex as prime virtues. According to the biography, Alfred struggled with this dichotomy of Christian life on the one hand and a more primal drive for glory (that included sin) on the other. In his later writings, Alfred asserted that he had been tempted during his youth by several different sins, noting that persevering had been very difficult. He stressed the difficulty of maintaining a healthy balance between the primal urges of the body and the more virtuous undertakings of the mind. A deep reading of Alfred's struggles identifies him not only as a Christian man who strived to be ideal but also as a righteous, Stoic-like man who tried to guide his way with morals.

Interestingly, young Alfred had visited Rome with his brother Æthelred in the year 853, sent there by their father, King Æthelwulf. The *Chronicle* mentions that Alfred was blessed as a future king by Pope Leo IV, and the story of their meeting is confirmed in other written sources. However, the *Chronicle* likely exaggerates when it asserts that the pope specifically blessed Alfred as a future king. Papal letters to King Æthelwulf mention Alfred as a "spiritual son" of the pope who was treated as a real "Roman consul," decorated with lavish garments and accessories.

Nevertheless, this meeting obviously would have helped push Alfred's agenda to present himself as a legitimate, Christian king during Wessex's chaotic political situation in the latter half of the ninth century. Alfred's visit to Rome is thus significant considering his future claims and behavior. It also provides insights into the earliest influences on young Alfred, as the confirmation of kingship by the pope was a profoundly Frankish Carolingian practice.

Whatever the case, Alfred's upbringing and early life played a very important role in the formation of his character, manifested in the policies he promoted throughout his reign. A prime example of this is his love of learning and belief that education was the long-term solution to Wessex's problems. Alfred recognized that education and literacy, together with true monastic tradition, had generally declined in the Anglo-Saxon kingdoms, as we noted earlier. Thus, to reverse this trend, Alfred decided to recruit distinguished scholars and monks to his court. Asser, his biographer from Wales, was among such recruits.

Alfred recognized that despite the importance of Latin as the primary language for learning in Europe at the time, its mastery in Anglo-Saxon lands was very low. He thus directed his reforms at making it easier, as well as necessary, for secular people to study and understand Latin. Translations of many important texts from Latin to Old English served this purpose.

Alfred believed that wisdom, curiosity, and knowledge were ideals that must be pursued by all individuals, including the nobility, who had largely neglected education in exchange for being involved in warfare, for example. He believed there were certain things all men must know, and he made this clear to the nobility.

The king used different tactics to encourage education among the West Saxon elites, even threatening to remove them from their privileged positions if they did not comply with his demands. This is not to say that he neglected all other aspects of the nobles' lives, such as their military skill and knowledge of warfare. We will see later that Alfred himself passed vital military reforms. Instead, he wanted knowledgeable people in his court because he believed it would allow him to make better decisions in all fields, including warfare. The way he saw it, the Crown had no use for uneducated and illiterate servants. Surely enough, in a few decades, an educated court would become a staple of monarchies throughout Europe.

There is no better example of Alfred's contributions to Christian kingship than his legal code. It served as an amalgamation of three legal codes that had come before his time—those of King Æthelbert of Kent, King Ine of Wessex, and King Offa of Mercia. From these previous documents, Alfred took the laws he believed to have been the most important and in need of repetition or clarification. Strictly speaking, there is little additional legal material in Alfred's code, but what it does not lack is Christian and Mosaic undertones.

This is especially apparent in the prologue, where it seems Alfred summarized the essence of the legal traditions of the Abrahamic religions. Providing an overview of Christian law-making at the beginning of the book heavily suggests that Alfred saw his code as a continuation of the tradition—as an essential part of what Christianity stood for. Thus, Alfred the Great's legal code serves as the primary example of an Anglo-Saxon king emphasizing the elements of Christian kingship. Though many had tried to impose this concept, few had succeeded to the level of Alfred's.

Alfred's reforms concerned more than the social and cultural aspects of West Saxon life in the late ninth century. His economic and military reforms were just as vital in making Wessex the newest most dominant Anglo-Saxon kingdom in Britain. These reforms must also be viewed relative to the political context: Alfred knew that his realm was in danger from the Great Heathen Army, and many of the changes were directed at combatting the immediate challenges the Vikings posed to Wessex's security and strength.

His monetary reform was implemented in 875, three years before he defeated the Vikings at Edington. The new West Saxon coinage, minted in Alfred's name throughout "greater Wessex," including London, had a fixed weight and a new design featuring classical Roman influences. What is more impressive is that the coinage reform was carried out with King Ceolwulf of Mercia—and it appears that Alfred was perceived as the "senior" king in this relationship. Many coins bear his name with the title of *Rex Anglorum*— "King of the Angles," or perhaps "King of the English," whereas Ceolwulf is simply mentioned as *rex*.

The fact that these coins were minted in non-traditionally West Saxon territories, such as London, suggests the increasing influence of Wessex over its neighbors by the middle of the 870s. A shared monetary system was key for Mercia and Wessex's economic and social integration, providing a great foundation for an eventual political union between the two kingdoms. The reform was very possibly Alfred's conscious attempt to expand his notion of universal kingship among the Anglo-Saxons. Imposing such an influence on the once-great state of Mercia, now torn by war and spared by Vikings, was the first move in asserting the new dominance of Wessex.

Alfred would gain more influence after the death of King Ceolwulf of Mercia, who was succeeded by an ealdorman named Æthelred in the late 870s. Æthelred ruled over the western part of Mercia still under Anglo-Saxon control but never enjoyed the title of "king," instead recognizing the overlordship of King Alfred. It appears that the two leaders had a mutual understanding, something that can be better seen after Æthelred married Alfred's daughter in the late 880s. Æthelred accepted Alfred as a superior political figure partially because the Vikings had weakened the Mercian position and partially because of Alfred's conscious efforts to transform the existing political relationship.

In addition to measures that altered the Anglo-Saxon economy by accelerating integration between Mercia and Wessex, Alfred took steps to significantly reform the Anglo-Saxon military. These changes were implemented in the face of the looming Viking threat that had identified clear shortcomings in the Anglo-Saxon strategies.

As we have mentioned, the Viking force's primary tactic was to avoid direct confrontation with the Anglo-Saxon armies. Often, the two sides would negotiate for the peaceful retreat of the Vikings in exchange for a sum of money or tribute, but the Vikings would often break these agreements and launch raids on other places. Thus, rather than their skill and ferocity in warfare, it was the adoption of smart tactics and the knowledge of their enemy's weaknesses—in this case, the inability of Anglo-Saxon kings to quickly muster up armies—that gave the Great Heathen Army a big advantage. It was less due to a discrepancy in the quality of the military, as Anglo-Saxon armies could defeat the Vikings when they intercepted them and forced an open battle.

Recognizing this problem, Alfred decided to split his army into two parts, creating a permanent standing force that could be mobilized much more quickly. The other half of the original army stayed in their homes and were not on active duty, but they could be mobilized if the Vikings attacked their residence or areas close by. If these pockets of local resistance could hold up the Vikings, the standing army could quickly provide support and ensure Anglo-Saxon victory.

Once the soldiers in the standing force had served for a certain amount of time, they would be replaced by soldiers who had stayed at home. This measure ensured not only a quick response to decentralized Viking attacks but also that the soldiers would always be fresh and ready for battle. Although communication problems rendered it difficult to coordinate when the standing army would be relieved, the West Saxon forces eventually adapted to the new system.

The final important reform Alfred implemented in the late 870s was the establishment of a network of defensive fortifications, known as burhs, at strategic locations throughout Wessex. The construction of defensive fortifications was nothing new for Britain, begun during the time of the Romans. In fact, some of Alfred's burhs were based on these older structures while others were placed in areas previously disregarded. The goal was to effectively cover all of Alfred's domains and dissuade concentrated Viking attacks in the future. Many fortifications were constructed on royal roads or at convenient locations on rivers to ensure that they restricted free Viking movement.

The burhs eventually grew, transforming the areas around them with new settlements. In a few centuries, many of them would become full-fledged towns with specialized industries and character, whereas others retained purely strategic importance. This reform, too, faced many difficulties. The most obvious was the costs of building and maintenance. A later document titled *Burghal Hidage* mentions that tens of thousands of men were needed to keep the system up and running. Evidence also suggests that Alfred did not complete the construction of several burh sites. Considering these challenges, it is even more impressive that the burh system built by Alfred persevered through time, expanded upon by future West Saxon kings.

All in all, King Alfred the Great of Wessex remains one of the most central figures of Anglo-Saxon history. He emerged as a leader against the Viking invasion and saved what remained of Anglo-Saxon kingdoms south of the Humber. His contributions to Anglo-Saxon resistance against the Great Heathen Army are certainly worthy of praise, and so are his policies as king. They are even more impressive when we consider that Alfred was acting primarily to preserve and protect his own kingdom. His later decisions, however, suggest that Alfred had a vision for the future of Anglo-Saxon kingship—a future he believed lay in integration, with Wessex as the leader. In fact, only two generations later, Alfred's grandson, Æthelstan would bear the title "King of the English" and be recognized as the first king of a united kingdom of England. Alfred was also instrumental in bringing back the tradition and love of learning to Medieval England. It is thanks to his efforts that we know so much about the history of the Anglo-Saxons.

Chapter Six – The Making of England

In this chapter, we will examine the fate of the Anglo-Saxons after the end of the Great Heathen Army invasion in the late ninth century. Previously, we looked at the reign of King Alfred of Wessex—the man commonly considered to have ended the Viking invasion of Anglo-Saxon England. His reforms not only kept the invaders in check but also laid the foundation for the future Kingdom of England. We also mentioned that Alfred's actions were not directed toward this unification, and the same can be said about his successors. As we will come to see, however, the decisions made by the succeeding rulers of Wessex would result in the creation of a unified Anglo-Saxons state. Below, we will take a closer look at the reigns of West Saxon kings such as Edward and Æthelstan and examine their actions within the wider perspective of early English nation-building. Given the unstable political circumstances of the age, examining the processes that led to Anglo-Saxon unification is even more compelling.

After Alfred

King Alfred died in October 899, succeeded by his son Edward, who would come to bear the title "the Elder." During his reign, Alfred was already referred to as the king of the Anglo-Saxons, and for good reason. Alfred's reign had brought much-needed stability to the Kingdom of Wessex, which had emerged as the most dominant of the remaining Anglo-Saxon kingdoms. However, this did not necessarily mean that his successors would likewise be recognized as over-kings.

In fact, the chaotic landscape of early tenth-century England added more complications to the existing power dynamics between the Anglo-Saxon kingdoms and the Vikings, who had firmly established themselves in eastern and northern England (the Danelaw). The Vikings had controlled territories both north and south of the Humber for decades before their possessions were recognized by Alfred. Since their invasion in 865, they had come to dominate the kingdoms of Northumbria and East Anglia and had emerged as overlords over much of Mercia. Their advance further south had only been stopped thanks to Alfred.

The Vikings' replacement of Anglo-Saxon political organization in the Danelaw remains obscure. In fact, the whole circumstance looked a lot like the arrival of the Anglo-Saxons in post-Roman Britain in the fifth century. Archeological findings from the time, the names of settlements, and genetic evidence clearly point to the increasing presence of the Vikings in these lands. It is unclear, however, whether an increasing number of Scandinavians, who were not necessarily warrior-explorers like traditional Vikings, continued to come to the Danelaw during the early ninth century. It is also possible that the Vikings who conquered these lands emerged as the new elite, replacing the existing Anglo-Saxon nobility through continued tribute collection.

There is also confusion about naming the territories conquered by the Vikings "the Danelaw." The first use of the term appears in eleventh-century sources, and it is unlikely it was used as a conscious distinction between different ethnic groups that made up Viking armies. "Danelaw" or "law of the Danes" suggests that for Anglo-Saxons, the Vikings were Danes, though the Great Heathen Army had contained warrior bands from different parts of Scandinavia. Thus, attributing a simpler term to a combination of Viking ethnicities, nationalities, or cultural identities (that were very similar, nevertheless) is not necessarily accurate. Still, the use of the term reflects the prominence of Scandinavian overlords in these lands.

We don't know how centralized the leadership of the Danelaw was or how connected this Viking realm was to Scandinavia. We can gather from contemporary West Saxon sources and archeological evidence that some form of cohesion existed among the different Viking warrior bands that had settled in the Danelaw. After the initial invasion of the Great Heathen Army, these warrior bands had most likely separated, drawn to different cities that they took over, like York, Nottingham, or Leicester. The *Anglo-Saxon Chronicle* mentions that the Danes had worked the lands they had conquered since the middle of the 870s, suggesting that the Vikings had intended to stay in this part of England. Having their authority over those lands recognized by Alfred in the 880s, the Vikings most likely did not feel the need to significantly alter their political organization in the Danelaw.

The Anglo-Saxons had remained in rough control of the northern part of Northumbria since the kingdom's conquest by the original wave of the Great Heathen Army, but they did not hold any considerable power. The southern lands of Northumbria were directly under the rule of the Vikings, who installed client kings in the northern part of the old kingdom to efficiently impose their rule on their subjects.

The situation was just as chaotic south of the Humber. East Anglia had been completely absorbed by the Vikings, whereas Sussex and Essex had been taken over by the Kingdom of Wessex. A significant part of Mercia had also been conquered by the Vikings, but the western half of the kingdom, commonly referred to as "English Mercia," remained under Anglo-Saxon rule and was politically dominated by Alfred throughout the later years of his reign.

All in all, these were the two significant axes of power in early tenth-century England: the Vikings, who ruled the lands of the Danelaw, and the Anglo-Saxon kingdoms of Wessex and Mercia, with West Saxon leadership. The political conflicts of the early tenth century mainly took place between these two powers.

The Kingdom of Wessex faced a succession struggle after the death of King Alfred in 899. Yes, his son Edward became king, but he was challenged by a person who had a rather serious claim to the West Saxon throne —Æthelwold, the younger son of King Æthelred and a nephew of King Alfred. Æthelwold had been an infant when his father died fighting the Vikings in 871, leading to the crown passing to his brother, Alfred. And though the *Chronicle* depicts a rather simple story of the transfer of power from Alfred to Edward, the events of the first years of the tenth century are very intriguing to examine.

It appears that Æthelwold, having come of age and perhaps aware of the fact that Alfred did not necessarily favor Edward as his successor, openly challenged Edward for the throne of Wessex. He had considerable support both inside Wessex and beyond its borders, though the *Chronicle,* written in the court of the eventual victor—Edward—mentions that Æthelwold's uprising was only an early rebellion swiftly dealt with by Edward.

In reality, Æthelwold sought military assistance from the Danes, who granted him this support, perhaps believing that Æthelwold would become another puppet king if he emerged successful. In the first years of the tenth century, Æthelwold incited the uprising of a large Viking force from East Anglia against Edward, who rushed there with an army to put an end to the challenger's prospects. Though the Danes under Æthelwold emerged victorious from the bloody Battle of the Holme in December of 902, Æthelwold died in battle, and his uprising subsequently ended.

It is also difficult to determine the extent of King Edward's power in the first years of his tenure. In the royal charters issued in his name, he is mentioned as the "King of the Anglo-Saxons," but it is unlikely that he exercised as much influence over English Mercia as his father had. The charters of King Æthelred of Mercia, who had recognized Alfred as overking since the 880s, do not mention Edward in the same manner. In fact, Mercian sources emphasize Æthelred's sovereignty as king and especially Æthelflæd—Alfred's daughter—as queen. In fact, sources such as the *Annals of Æthelflæd* and *Mercian Register* depict the queen as a very strong ruler herself, especially after the death of her husband in 911, acting independently and pursuing policies that would benefit Mercia.

Mercian coinage, on the other hand, tells a different story. It is issued in Edward's name, suggesting that Mercia was, at least nominally, under his control. It seems that though Edward exercised some form of power over Mercia, even taking command of Mercian forces in a campaign in 909, Mercian kings were relatively free to operate in their domains in the first few years of the tenth century.

After Æthelred's death in 911, Edward's rule over Mercia became firmer. He inherited some of the most important Mercian centers, such as London and Oxford, which greatly strengthened his position. From this point on, Edward also developed a better relationship with his sister Æthelflæd of Mercia, and it is plausible that the two coordinated their most important political decisions in the following years. The fruits of this relationship were manifested in the joint policies against the Vikings throughout the Danelaw. These policies included not only offensive military campaigns in East Anglia and eastern parts of Mercia but also the continued construction of key defensive burhs in territories still controlled by the Anglo-Saxons to keep the borders safe. The royal charters from this time refer to the Vikings of East Anglia and Northumbria as two separate armies and political entities, suggesting that the leadership of the Danelaw was decentralized.

The construction of burhs made it difficult for Vikings to cross into the West Saxon or Mercian countryside and pillage the lands. Over time, they were constructed closer to the border between the dominions of the Anglo-Saxons and the Danelaw, such as at Hertford and Witham in Essex. These defenses were set up to check potential Viking offensives from East Anglia into the lands north of the Thames River, those that led directly to London, which was a crucial center of power. The burh network spread out like a spiderweb, each supporting the next and enabling the whole system to be sustainable.

It appears that this policy was soon relatively successful. Burhs constructed in the English heartlands eventually caused some Viking centers to submit to the Anglo-Saxon rulers of Mercia and Wessex.

By 918, most of the large cities south of the Humber thus appear to have submitted to the Anglo-Saxons, with individual Viking leaders striking agreements and offering to pledge their allegiance. Because of the lack of West Saxon charters in this period, it is difficult to determine what exactly caused such a shift in political organization. However, evidence suggests that the most elite Vikings likely kept their estates after pleading with Edward. It is thus likely that gradual West Saxon and Mercian military domination forced the Viking leaders to submit one by one, though this was done carefully to keep the peace instead of exploiting Viking trust. The Danes, who saw benefits in aligning with the kingdoms of Mercia and Wessex, thus negotiated on behalf of their subjects. We know that this large-scale transfer of the Danelaw lands south of the Humber into Edward's control was a profound process because of the coins minted in the West Saxon king's name.

With the death of Æthelflæd in 918, Edward was essentially the most powerful Anglo-Saxon king, and he proceeded to quickly assert his power over Mercia. The *Anglo-Saxon Chronicle* mentions him pushing to the site of the queen's death at Tamworth in Staffordshire, where the Mercian people decided to submit to him, along with three Welsh rulers, who had probably been under Æthelflæd's influence. Edward then took Ælfwynn, the daughter of the late Mercian queen, to Wessex, perhaps to deal with the potential threat of a succession challenger sooner rather than later. This incident essentially gave Edward a level of control over Mercia similar to his father Alfred's, once again uniting two of the strongest Anglo-Saxon kingdoms.

Moreover, in the next two to three years, Edward continued his policy of "defensive expansion" by constructing burhs all around his realm. In this way, he made his control of the vast Mercian territories firmer, even making advances in the Northumbrian Danelaw territories. The *Chronicle* remarks that Edward was chosen as the "father and lord" not only by the English and the Danes south of the Humber but also by Ragnald of York, the prominent Viking leader of the northern Danelaw. The exact circumstances surrounding Edward being chosen as overlord are unclear, but it suggests that Ragnald struck a mutual recognition treaty with Edward in which he retained control of York and surrounding territories north of the Humber.

On the other hand, Edward was recognized as the sole leader of the Anglo-Saxons, who were starting to be called the "English." The reigns of Alfred and Edward had done a lot for this important identity transformation, which would be finalized during the reign of Edward's successor.

The King of the English

Historians disagree on the nature of Anglo-Saxon nation-building or unification, and the prominent stance is that it was never consciously initiated. Anglo-Saxon rulers, ever since they could be called kings and their realms in Britain called kingdoms, were motivated by personal gain. Anglo-Saxon kings were aware of their tough political environment, and increasing political power at the expense of others was always the chief motivation behind the reigns of kings such as Offa of Mercia or Alfred of Wessex. These rulers were great because they could adapt to changing circumstances and emerge from extremely challenging times as dominant figures. This is true even though these rulers were often referred to as "over-kings" or "kings of the Anglo-Saxons" or "kings of Britain."

There are also complications in defining "unity" among the Anglo-Saxons. What exactly does this word entail when we consider the complex ethnic, linguistic, and cultural makeup of the British Isles during the Middle Ages? Where exactly did the Anglo-Saxon realms end? How could a ruler be objectively considered the king of the Anglo-

Saxons? Better yet, how could a ruler be considered the king of the English?

Thus, when we speak of King Æthelstan of Wessex as the first king of the English after 927, we must clear up all this confusion, especially because Æthelstan did not directly inherit all the territories previously controlled by his father Edward. The events immediately following Edward's death in 924 remain unclear, but it seems that Æthelstan initially only succeeded him in Mercia, whereas his brother Ælfweard inherited the throne of Wessex. We don't know whether Edward had divided the lands between his sons before his death. This explanation is valid, as Frankish kings in Europe had practiced this way of succession for quite a while.

Ælfweard may also have been proclaimed king in Wessex because Edward had died in Mercian territories, where he had been accompanied by Æthelstan, who had a history of being involved in Mercian affairs. For example, Æthelstan had participated in the campaigns with his aunt and uncle, Æthelflæd and Æthelred, and was more known to the Mercian court. However, Ælfweard died less than three weeks after Edward. Æthelstan thus became the king of both Mercia and Wessex, though he initially faced minor resistance in Wessex when he tried to impose his power. Importantly, he was proclaimed king in September of 925 at Kingston-upon-Thames—a place chosen specifically because of its location on the border between Wessex and Mercia.

Frontispiece of Bede's Life of St Cuthbert, showing King Æthelstan presenting a copy of the book to the saint himself.
https://commons.wikimedia.org/wiki/File:Athelstan_(cropped).jpg

Æthelstan ruled for about fifteen years until his death in 939, which makes his great achievement of English unification that much more impressive. By the time of his accession to the throne, the only major Anglo-Saxon realm not under his rulership was Danish Northumbria, centered around the city of York. (Previous West Saxon and Mercian kings had already regained control of East Anglia and eastern Mercian territories.) Æthelstan became the first southern Anglo-Saxon ruler of Northumbria, as well. He managed this through a marriage alliance between his sister and Sihtric, the Viking ruler of York, in 926.

Sihtric, who had previously also ruled the Viking-controlled Kingdom of Dublin, had become the King of York in 921 after the death of Ragnald of York. The Danish ruler's position may have been weakened due to his prior wars with the Brittonic kingdoms of the north, forcing him to negotiate with Æthelstan.

Importantly, Sihtric died only about a year after marrying Æthelstan's sister, and the *Chronicle* mentions that it was the West Saxon king who "succeeded the kingdom of the Northumbrians." It is difficult to grasp the extent to which Æthelstan was initially accepted by the Northumbrian people as their king, but he may have been first challenged by Guthfrith, a cousin of Sihtric who led a small force from Dublin. This resistance was unprepared and fell short of preventing Æthelstan from imposing his power in York, however.

Crucially, other northern kings also submitted to Æthelstan at Eamont in July 927. Among them were King Constantine of Alba (Scotland) and King Owain of the Brittonic Kingdom of Strathclyde. Additionally, the Welsh also accepted Æthelstan's overlordship. The Welsh kingdoms of Gwent, Deheubarth, and Gwynedd had proclaimed their allegiance to the Mercian and West Saxon kings at the beginning of the tenth century and extended it to Æthelstan, as well. All these rulers appeared as witnesses in Æthelstan's royal charters for the next several years and regularly attended the West Saxon court, residing there as the most respected figures. This confirms the extent of the overlordship and influence Æthelstan had achieved in the first three to four years of his reign.

Æthelstan's control of Northumbria was by no means firm, however. The Northumbrians had always considered themselves separate from other Anglo-Saxon kingdoms and had a special identity. This had been the first time a ruler from south of the Humber had successfully imposed his rule on Northumbria, and Æthelstan was rightfully faced with dissent.

To improve his standing in Northumbria, Æthelstan made generous land grants to different nobles and members of the clergy.

But the question of the territories at the border between Northumbria and the Scottish domains in the north complicated the matters. These lands, formerly part of the old Kingdom of Bernicia, had been under the control of Ealdred of Bamburgh until his death in 934. That year, Æthelstan launched a northern invasion, going farther than any other Anglo-Saxon king had previously campaigned. The reason for the invasion is unclear, but a conflict between King Constantine of Alba and Æthelstan after the death of Ealdred is a possibility. Together with Æthelstan were the Welsh rulers who had pledged their allegiance to Æthelstan, suggesting that his influence was tangible at this time.

According to the *Chronicle,* Scotland was attacked both on land and by sea, though the exact details of the campaign—and, more importantly, its outcome—are also shrouded in mystery. We know that Æthelstan was back in Buckingham in central England later that year, issuing a charter in which Constantine was referred to as a sub-king. In later charters, however, beginning from 935, Constantine no longer appears as a witness, while all the other kings who had pledged loyalty to Æthelstan were still mentioned.

The strained relationship between Æthelstan and Constantine escalated into a full-scale conflict a few years later. The *Chronicle* records that a decisive battle took place in 937 at Brunanburh (whose exact location has not been determined) between West Saxons under King Æthelstan and a combined force of Scots under King Constantine, Britons of Strathclyde under King Owain, and Vikings from Dublin under King Olaf Guthfrithson.

Olaf had succeeded his father three years earlier as King of Dublin and had allied with the Scots after marrying Constantine's daughter. Possibly, his campaign from Ireland into northern England was his bid for the throne of York, which he believed had been unjustly lost to Æthelstan.

The allied forces launched an invasion in late 937 but were eventually defeated at Brunanburh by Æthelstan in a bloody battle. There were many casualties on both sides, including important family members of the kings involved in the battle. Æthelstan's victory was seen as decisive, and a poem was dedicated to him in the *Chronicle* to celebrate his achievement. As we will see, however, the question of the dominance of English kings in Northumbria would remain largely unresolved until years after the death of Æthelstan.

Æthelstan was thus the first King of the English, ruling over the lands that had been taken over by the Anglo-Saxon migrants after the end of Roman rule in Britain. But he was also more than that. He was the strongest political leader in the British Isles. He exacted tribute from the Welsh and received their military assistance; he had successfully subdued the Brittonic kingdoms of the north and the Vikings from Dublin. In some of his charters, Æthelstan is referred to as "emperor," and this notion is not far from reality. The House of Wessex was the most powerful royal house in Britain at the time.

Æthelstan's reign was the period in the Anglo-Saxon history of England when the royal court was most involved with European affairs. Through royal marriages and frequent involvement with European leaders, Æthelstan provided a great example for other tenth-century Anglo-Saxon rulers. For example, to bolster his international reputation and legitimacy, Æthelstan pursued a friendly foreign policy with the Franks. After the dissolution of the Carolingian Empire, the rival royal families descended from Charlemagne also sought legitimacy and influence. It is in this light that the marriage between Eadgyth, the half-sister of Æthelstan, and the soon-to-be Emperor Otto of the Holy Roman Empire should be viewed.

Æthelstan is not just remembered for his conquest of Northumbria and his privileged position as the most powerful ruler in Britain. He was also a great reformer and strengthened the domestic legal and administrative framework of his kingdom. Æthelstan was faced with new challenges as the first Anglo-Saxon king to rule such a vast piece of territory, close to the modern borders of England. He decided to centralize his rule to govern more effectively. He produced the most legal texts and royal charters of any ruler to make the practice an inherent part of kingship and thus legitimize his rule in all Anglo-Saxon lands. He also held frequent councils and moved from one city to another. These councils, known as witans, were a crucial part of Æthelstan's administration. Officials of different ranks, members of the clergy, nobles, ealdormen, and many other figures usually attended and discussed relevant affairs. It can be argued that this practice played a big role in the parliamentarian tradition modern England is known for today.

Æthelstan also understood that he was a Christian king. He knew that he had to carefully choose his actions and cultivate good relations with the Church. During his reign, the clergy played an important role in creating and spreading new laws, most of which were based on other great Anglo-Saxon codes, such as Alfred's. Æthelstan consulted regularly with Archbishop Wulfhelm of Canterbury, who drew up many of the laws concerning royal relations with the Church.

Overall, Christianity became more prominent in the English laws during Æthelstan's reign, and the fusion of the two aspects of life became a staple of Medieval European kingdoms. His four codes issued at Grately, Exeter, Faversham, and Thunderfield address a wide range of social and economic hardships that might have been prominent at the time. They are concerned with matters such as the failure to pay tithes to the Church, thievery, the possession and exchange of property, and the procession of justice affairs. Æthelstan's laws were extensive and ambitious, demonstrating his commitment to impose and maintain order in challenging circumstances.

Æthelstan was also one of the most pious and educated Anglo-Saxon kings. Again, in this respect, he built on the foundations laid by his grandfather, Alfred the Great. For example, the fact that Æthelstan continued to issue laws in the vernacular Old English shows Alfred's influence, and so does his patronage of culture.

Importantly, the archbishopric of Canterbury had come under direct West Saxon control by the time Æthelstan became king, and he used this position to increase his leverage over the Church. Throughout West Saxon lands, for example, the king exerted the most influence in religious matters, even promoting and appointing loyal bishops to different dioceses.

Æthelstan also did a great deal to better integrate the Church of Northumbria into his realm, as it had developed separately since the invasion of the Vikings. Many monasteries and churches were founded in the lands formerly controlled by the Danes to combat the possible backsliding of Christian values in these areas. He was especially involved with the cult of Saint Cuthbert, the patron saint of Northumbria, located in Durham, to which he graciously donated many times during his reign, including during his northern campaign. Among his donations was a copy of Bede's *Life of Saint Cuthbert*, written entirely in Old English and featuring an illustration of Æthelstan presenting the book to the saint.

In general, Æthelstan donated extensively to different religious institutions all around his kingdom and beyond it, forging relations with foreign bishops throughout Europe. He also avidly collected ancient relics and old manuscripts, many of which he gifted to various monastic establishments. His commitment to these matters was mimicked by his successors, and ecclesiastic revival can be considered a characteristic of tenth-century England. No doubt, political motivations lay behind Æthelstan's actions, but they nevertheless resulted in a rich and rare cultural legacy in a time of great turmoil.

The House of Wessex

Æthelstan, the first King of the English, united all the lands of the Anglo-Saxons, ending years of Viking dominance in Northumbria and making all the rival kings of Britain submit to him. However, though his reign was overwhelmingly positive for the kingdom, problems started to appear after Æthelstan's death at the young age of about 45 in 939. The most obvious problem Æthelstan's successors faced was keeping the north in check. The Northumbrians' historical reluctance to accept southerners as kings, paired with a renewed Viking interest in controlling York and its surrounding territories, complicated matters for kings Edmund and Eadred.

Edmund, brother of Æthelstan, ascended the throne with no difficulties in 939, but his authority in Northumbria was very quickly challenged by a familiar figure—Olaf Guthfrithson, who returned with a small force from Dublin in 940. The people of York proclaimed Olaf as king, and he proceeded to turn his attention to the English heartlands. He directed his efforts to taking the "Five Boroughs"—the important centers of Nottingham, Lincoln, Derby, Leicester, and Stamford—all located in eastern Mercia. He was endorsed in this endeavor by Archbishop Wulfstan of York, whose motivations for supporting Olaf remain unclear.

King Edmund finally confronted the Danish leader at Leicester, but he was unsuccessful in his siege and was forced to recognize Olaf as the ruler of the area. Only after the death of Olaf two years later did Edmund successfully reconquer the "Five Boroughs" and drive out the Norsemen who had returned to eastern Mercia with Olaf's offensive. In 944, the reconquest of Northumbria was completed when Edmund took back York from Olaf's brother Ragnald and another Viking leader, Olaf Sihtricson. After Edmund's death in May 946 and the succession of his brother Eadred as the new king, Northumbria was again lost, this time to the legendary Viking Eric Bloodaxe, who would not be driven out until 954.

Despite these hardships throughout the 940s and the 950s, with Northumbria and eastern Mercia repeatedly targeted by the Vikings, the development of social, economic, administrative, and cultural processes in England never ceased. The progress in these fields showed during the reign of King Edgar, nicknamed "the Peaceful" because of the relative lack of military activities during his almost sixteen-year tenure as king, starting in 959. Edgar had ruled Mercia since the death of his father in 955 and inherited the southern part of the kingdom from his brother, Eadwig, after his death.

King Edgar largely followed policies like those of his predecessors, continuing to assert firm rule over Northumbria and expanding on the legal framework. By the time he became king, the West Saxon model of governance had already become very mature, with a clearly defined administrative body that delegated the legal authority of some of the most powerful noble families and ealdormen.

The laws issued during the era of the House of Wessex had already introduced changes to taxation based on the "system of hundreds"—a new unit of land division. By the end of his reign, Edgar had also transformed the monetary system of his kingdom, centralizing the production and distribution of coins and introducing a new dimension of unity that is a testament to his rule in all the Anglo-Saxon realms.

More importantly, however, the ecclesiastical society of England underwent a profound transformation during the tenth century, with the leading figures of the Church making important changes that were endorsed by the king. Three religious figures were at the head of these changes—Archbishop Dunstan of Canterbury, Bishop Æthelwold of Winchester, and Archbishop Oswald of York. Our knowledge of these reforms comes almost entirely from biased sources, mostly biographies produced after Edgar's reign. Nevertheless, texts from the latter half of the tenth century are dominated by religious accounts, where the main motivations for the reforms are spelled out. It appears that the reformers sought to reverse the alleged decline of monastic life in England that had taken place after the Viking invasions.

The reformers were also heavily influenced by Bede's *Ecclesiastical History*, which criticized the Anglo-Saxon religious practices, and the ongoing continental monastic reform movement. They argued, much like their European contemporaries during the tenth century, that the English Church had fallen into disarray, with monasteries populated by clergy who had families and owned extensive property. Instead, the reformers believed that the clergy should live their lives according to the Rule of St. Benedict—in celibacy and with full focus on religious activities.

The contacts the English kings had forged with Christian kingdoms (and, therefore, with Christian clergy in Europe) certainly amplified these sentiments. The reforms were mostly pushed in the monasteries of Wessex and Mercia, where, by the year 975, many Benedictine-style monasteries and nunneries had been established. The religious officials, with support from the Crown, often confiscated the possessions of clergy who lived in the old monasteries, driving them out and installing monks and nuns in their place to keep the institutions running. Edgar expressed his support by granting numerous donations to new monasteries, further boosting interest and activity.

In 970, the reformers introduced laws that imposed uniform rules on all Benedictine monasteries in the kingdom to avoid diverging from the original rule book, which was translated into Old English and widely distributed to boost its appeal and reach. The enforcement of uniformity can be seen as a major political move to assert the unity of a kingdom ruled by one king. Still, the reformers encountered many difficulties in enforcing the reforms, especially in Northumbria, where monastic life did not change as significantly.

The leaders of the reforms had also been Edgar's close political allies since the king's youth, supporting his claim to the throne after the death of his brother, Eadwig. If looked at in this sense, the Benedictine reforms in England in the tenth century were also directed toward increasing the influence of these religious officials in the royal court. By the late tenth century, the Benedictine reform movement in England had not only greatly affected the ecclesiastical affairs in religious institutions throughout the kingdom but also strengthened the position of the Crown. As we will come to see, despite these changes, the authority of later West Saxon kings would be put to the test in the final decades of the millennium.

Chapter Seven – From Æthelred the Unready to William the Conqueror

In the final chapter of the book, we will look at the later history of the Anglo-Saxons, starting with the reign of Æthelred, who has been given the title "the Unready" because of the troubled nature of his rule. As we will come to see, Æthelred would be unable to maintain stability in the kingdom because of many different domestic and external factors that plagued his reign. The late tenth century would also bring a renewed wave of large-scale Viking invasions, which eventually crippled the power of the West Saxon kings and forced them to adapt to changing political circumstances. New Viking activity would even result in the expulsion of the House of Wessex and the emergence of Scandinavian rulers on the English throne for several decades. This chaotic part of Anglo-Saxon history ended with a succession struggle in the mid-eleventh century, when a seemingly unlikely bid succeeded the throne of England, marking a new era in the history of the Anglo-Saxons. We will dive deep and analyze the complex procession of events from Æthelred's accession to William of Normandy's conquest of England in 1066. Finally, we will assess the era of Anglo-Saxon dominance in Britain and the material and cultural legacy with which the Anglo-Saxons are remembered in history.

Æthelred the Unready

The reign of King Æthelred the Unready, from 978 until 1016, including a brief interregnum caused by his overthrow and return in 1013-1014. It is generally considered one of the low points of Anglo-Saxon kingship, and not just because it led to the collapse of the House of Wessex's power. Contemporary and later chroniclers note a complete degradation of England's socio-political and economic spheres at the time, no doubt accelerated by a renewed wave of Viking invasions from Scandinavia. These invasions, which increased in severity throughout the 990s and reached their peak in the first decade of the eleventh century, took a great toll on the English king, who failed to maintain the unity of his kingdom and was forced to abandon his subjects.

In short, King Æthelred was given the nickname "the Unready" for many reasons. Certainly, his inability and weakness of character contributed to the decline of his kingdom's power. Upon closer observation, however, Æthelred's reign appears to have been troubled with problems from the outset—problems rooted deep in the nature of the Anglo-Saxon society of the late tenth century.

To understand the troubles that plagued Æthelred's reign, it is important to look at the events of the second half of the 970s that led to him becoming king. Æthelred's father, King Edgar the Peaceful, died in July 975, and the *Chronicle* describes his death as a great tragedy —a sentiment that undoubtedly stems from the king's religious inclinations and his patronage of the monastic reforms during his reign. The people mourned the death of a beloved leader who had guaranteed them peace and security for the fifteen years he had been king.

However, powerful individuals, such as Ealdorman Ælfhere of Mercia, used the chaos provided by Edgar's death to reclaim lands the Church had gained during his reign by forcefully expelling monks and nuns from religious institutions. In the *Life of St. Oswald*, the biographer notes a widespread crackdown on monks and monasteries previously under Edgar's patronage in an event that historians have deemed the "anti-monastic reaction."

This reaction was not necessarily against the new form of monasticism and Christian practice since those who seized the moment were benefactors of the Church. Instead, it appears to have been a move to reclaim some of the political power that had been undermined by the prominent leaders of the Church during Edgar's reign. Some nobles, for instance, justified their actions by claiming that they had been coerced into giving up their lands to the Church to comply with the king's new regulations.

It was in this chaos that Edward, son of Edgar and his first wife, Æthelflæd (who was thirteen years old at the time), ascended the throne. This was largely made possible thanks to the influence of friends in his father's court, such as Archbishop Dunstan of Canterbury. Unexpectedly, however, the young king was mysteriously murdered in March 978—less than three years after he ascended to the throne—during a visit to his half-brother, Æthelred, the son of King Edgar from his second wife, Ælfthryth. Edward, tragically murdered in unclear circumstances, was venerated as a martyr. It was another tragedy, one that called into question the integrity of the reign of Æthelred, crowned king less than two weeks later. Æthelred, himself four years younger than Edward, may have been an ignorant victim of the intrigues of the royal court.

Æthelred's rule was unique. As king, he was characterized by his contemporaries and later writers as weak, passive, and largely unsuccessful, influenced by various interest groups and never quite able to assert authority over his most powerful subjects. The *Chronicle* tells of his inability to control the Anglo-Saxon nobility, his tendency to make impulsive and violent decisions, and his naivety when dealing with the Vikings.

As we mentioned, it was the combination of all these factors that gave him the title "the Unready." However, the sources that provide the most detailed accounts of Æthelred's reign, like the C, D, and E versions of the *Anglo-Saxon Chronicle*, were compiled after it had ended, in the court of a rival king—Cnut the Great. Because these accounts are not contemporary, they are inherently biased due to their knowledge of the disastrous nature of Æthelred's tenure as king. Thus, when speaking of Æthelred, it is important to counterbalance these sources with primary accounts produced by the king's contemporaries, such as the A version of the *Chronicle,* though such sources contain much fewer details.

A depiction of Æthelred the Unready.
https://commons.wikimedia.org/wiki/File:Ethelred_the_Unready.jpg

In the second half of the 980s Æthelred appears to have gained more influence in the kingdom's political affairs. Early in his reign, he was the victim of court rivalries between different interest groups, including ones stemming from the monastic reform and its reaction after Edgar's death. The names of some of the most powerful figures that had dominated the witness lists of the royal charters for the first few years of Æthelred's disappeared in the 980s. Some, like Bishop Æthelwold of Winchester, died (in his case, 984). The disappearance of other names from the royal charters, like Queen Mother Ælfthryth, suggests their influence or power had declined.

By 985, King Æthelred appears to have also issued his first law code and regained control of centralized coin minting. Charters from this time show a shift in policy and preferences for choosing allies. Æthelred granted a lot of land back to the Church as a conscious effort to recoup its losses during the anti-monastic reaction. Thus, in about ten years, Æthelred partially overcame the influential figures of the old system and undermined their interests in favor of new groups with whom he began to build personal relationships. However, by this time, King Æthelred was faced with a threat that significantly affected his decisions and forced him to appropriate many resources to keeping his kingdom secure.

Though the Danish influence had been significantly reduced in England since the reign of Æthelstan, not all the Danes had been forced to leave England with the conquest of Northumbria. As we remarked earlier, most Danes, now Christians, were well-integrated into the kingdom. It certainly seemed that the Vikings had been largely dealt with. The raids that took place in the early 980s were very localized and small in scale. In fact, there is no reason to suspect that Viking activity of this scale had completely ceased during the tenth century, as Viking realms had persevered in parts of Britain and Ireland. Despite catching the English by surprise at places like Southampton, Devon, Portland, or Cornwall during this period, the Vikings were quickly driven back.

This pattern of small-scale Viking raids on the English coastal areas changed in 991 when a large raiding party of ninety ships sailed to England from Norway, led by Olaf Tryggvason—the future Norwegian king. This force targeted important areas in Essex, pillaging towns such as Ipswich before confronting an English army at the Battle of Maldon in August. We don't have many details about how the battle played out, but we know that it ended in a Viking victory, with the English ealdorman and leader of the army—Byrhtnoth—slain in the field. King Æthelred was forced to negotiate and supposedly paid off the Vikings with a huge sum of 10,000 pounds to stop their attacks before proceeding to build up his fleet to catch the treacherous Vikings. However, he was betrayed by one of his ealdormen, who let the invaders escape.

The raid of 991 was the first of many destructive large-scale Viking attacks that were to come for the next two decades. Olaf Tryggvason returned in 994 with a similar-sized force, accompanied by Sweyn "Forkbeard" of Denmark, first attacking London and then targeting the coasts of Essex and Sussex. The Vikings were paid off once again, this time with gold and silver worth 16,000 pounds. As a guarantee that they would stop the attack, Olaf Tryggvason converted to Christianity and sailed back to Scandinavia. The amounts paid to the Vikings in exchange for peace were huge sums, and the *Chronicle* mentions that these kinds of payments continued well into the first decade of the eleventh century. The accounts are likely exaggerated, especially as it would have been virtually impossible to collect coins worth this much. The amount paid to the Viking armies probably included a large portion of valuables, such as relics from churches or other forms of booty.

Tribute was not just paid to the Vikings in exchange for peace. Sometimes, the English hired soldiers from the Viking army as mercenaries, with the agreement that they would defend the English shores from other Viking attacks. All in all, it was a widespread solution, practiced well before Æthelred became king. It was often pursued separately by local officials to keep their lands safe. Still, despite the best efforts of the English, these measures would not be enough to dissuade further Viking raids, which intensified in the late 990s and caused great destruction and turmoil.

The House of Denmark

Viking attacks continued with more ferocity in 997, three years after Æthelred had struck a peace deal with the previous army. The invaders first pillaged the shores of southwestern England, moving around for the following two years before raiding Normandy in the year 1000. Another force also attacked Sussex and later Devon the following year.

All these attacks had forced King Æthelred to adapt his policies, but it was becoming clear that resisting such fast-paced invasions would be a challenging task—one that required cooperation from local leaders. The *Chronicle* mentions that some ealdormen, such as Ulfcetel of East Anglia, were defeated in 1004 when they tried to confront the raiding Vikings. Others were reluctant to commit their forces to the costly struggle against the Scandinavians. Duke Richard of Normandy was ready to cooperate with the English, having agreed to mutual peace and a defensive alliance against the Vikings in 991. This alliance was reconfirmed when Æthelred married Richard's daughter, Emma, in 1002. The need to search for new allies confirms that the Viking raids were a significant threat at this time.

While Æthelred's decision to ally with the Normans can be justified, the same cannot be said of his policies for dealing with the Vikings in his realm. The "Saint Brice's Day Massacre"—arguably the most infamous event of Æthelred's reign—took place in November 1002. The king, in a decision that appears to be that of a paranoid ruler, ordered all Danish men in England to be killed, believing they had been conspiring with the invading Vikings to overthrow him. This decree was likely directed toward Danes who had recently settled in England as opposed to those who had lived in the kingdom for generations, by now well assimilated with the Anglo-Saxons. Perhaps, Æthelred wanted to eliminate the Scandinavian mercenaries who had agreed to fight with the English, as there were instances when they had been disloyal. Archeological evidence of mass graves containing the skulls of tens of males with Scandinavian genes, unearthed at Dorset and Oxford in the 2000s, has been identified as proof that the massacre did indeed take place.

A large army returned from Scandinavia in the year 1009, led by a Danish commander named Thorkell, who had accompanied Sweyn Forkbeard in his previous raids. This invasion proved to be too much for Æthelred, who had been struggling with endless court intrigue. We know that the king had lost the support of some of his most powerful allies, including the nobility and ealdormen of various provinces, because they no longer appeared in his charters as witnesses at the beginning of the eleventh century. Æthelred had tried to prepare for an impending Viking attack by commissioning the construction of a large English naval force, but this project had faced many setbacks, prone to corruption and betrayal.

Thorkell's army, when it landed in Kent in 1009, was paid off by the local ruler and made its way into Sussex, where it mercilessly ravaged the English countryside for the next few months. The English were unable to strike back, leading the Vikings to sack Canterbury in 1011 and take Archbishop Ælfheah (who was later murdered) prisoner. Æthelred was then forced to pay a ridiculous sum of money as a tribute—the *Chronicle* says 48,000 pounds of gold and silver—as part of the peace agreement with Thorkell. The Viking leader not only agreed to send his soldiers home and cease attacks on England but also joined Æthelred with a force of forty-five ships.

A year later, Sweyn Forkbeard, now king of both Denmark and Norway, returned with a large force and launched a full-scale invasion of England, making his way from Kent to the East Midlands. What happened next was an almost instant collapse of whatever power Æthelred had maintained. English ealdormen refused to fight the Vikings under Thorkell. One by one, the lands of England fell to the invaders, like dominoes. The "Five Boroughs" submitted to Sweyn with little resistance—a thorn in the side of Æthelred, who tried to resist the invaders. With the help of Thorkell, Æthelred put up a fight at London but could not chase the Vikings to inflict decisive casualties. Sweyn moved west, pillaging the countryside until Æthelmær's surrender, which eventually forced the king to surrender London as well. In late 1013, Æthelred was forced into exile in Normandy.

The Scandinavian king only lasted as the king of England for a few months before suffering an unexpected death in February 1014. Naturally, his army declared his son, Cnut, as the new king. The Anglo-Saxon nobility, however, who had submitted to Sweyn during his conquests, were reluctant to accept his son as their new overlord. Instead, they "invited" Æthelred back to be king again. This invitation was likely based on certain demands from the nobles, who had reasons to feel mistreated or undermined. The *Chronicle* mentions that they made Æthelred promise to solve his previous mistakes and grant amnesty to those who had betrayed him the previous year. Thus, in hindsight, Æthelred's return to the throne was doomed from the beginning. Nevertheless, he accepted.

Hearing this, Cnut was forced to flee back to Scandinavia. Æthelred, however, could not hold on to the power or authority that would guarantee the loyalty of his subjects. He proceeded to campaign in Lincolnshire, punishing the nobles who had supported Sweyn. This resulted in yet another rebellion, this time led by his own son, Edmund "Ironside."

Edmund established himself in the north, where anti-Æthelred sentiments had been the strongest, and quickly gained local support. Edmund was likely motivated by his desire to gain the throne for himself because he had been disregarded as a potential successor by Æthelred in favor of Edmund's half-brother, Edward. Edward, the son of Æthelred by his second wife Emma of Normandy and a teenager at this time, was already starting to be involved in political affairs beside his father.

Edmund's bid for power, however, was also short-lived. Cnut returned to England after having replenished his forces in Denmark and took the fight directly to the territories of Wessex. Æthelred was not ready to confront the returning Vikings as he had fallen ill, and Edmund led the resistance this time. Just like his father, however, his allies, including Thorkell, defected to the enemy.

Æthelred died in April 1016 as Cnut was pillaging the lands of England and negotiating terms of peace with local nobles. At the Battle of Assandun, fought in October 1016 (the exact location of which has not been determined), Cnut decisively defeated Edmund's forces and forced him to surrender. The two leaders agreed to divide the Kingdom of England, with Edmund only retaining control of the lands of Wessex. This division did not last long, however. Edmund died a month later, and Cnut assumed control of England. He was now the king of Denmark, Norway, and England, a political entity referred to as the North Sea Empire. The House of Wessex, which had united and ruled England for over a century, had fallen.

Perhaps because he was a foreign king or the lack of royal charters produced during his nineteen years as king of England, we are left with the sense that the reigns of Cnut and his two successors from the House of Denmark were a transitory period. This is partially due to the events of 1066, which ended the dominance of this dynasty that ruled the North Sea Empire.

By all means, Cnut was one of the most powerful rulers England had ever seen—and certainly the most competent and experienced since at least Edgar the Peaceful. England had been at its lowest as he ascended the throne of England in 1016 and, as a foreigner with a history of hostility with the English, he had to do a lot of work to reverse the decline of English power. The policies adopted during his reign, as well as the fact that it marked a brief period of relative peace in England, testify that he achieved stability in a complex environment. The fact that he is one of those rulers with the title "the Great" also supports this.

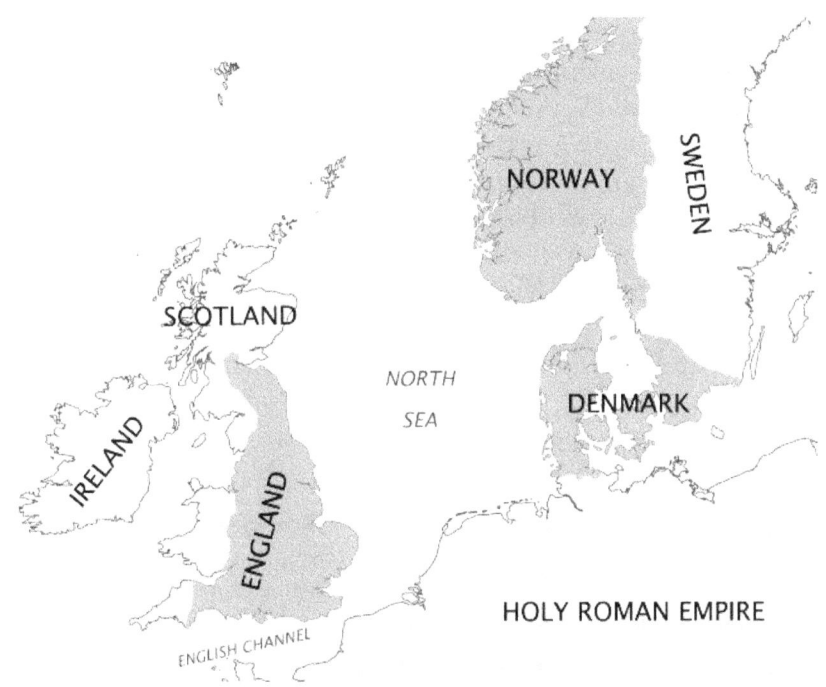

A map of Cnut's North Seas empire.
Hel-hama, CC BY-SA 3.0 <https://creativecommons.org/licenses/by-sa/3.0>, via Wikimedia Commons; https://commons.wikimedia.org/wiki/File:Cnut_lands.svg

As King of England, Denmark, and Norway during an age when it took information weeks to be delivered from one place to another, Cnut found himself in a rather unique position in 1016. He realized the need to adopt several measures that would ensure the safety of his position in England, especially as he was often absent, busy attending to matters in Scandinavia, such as domestic rebellions. To strengthen his control over England, Cnut divided the lands he had conquered into four parts, assigning each to one of his supporters in 1017. He kept control of Wessex, delegating East Anglia to Thorkell, Northumbria to Erik of Hlathir, and Mercia to Eadric Streona.

In addition, Cnut eliminated resistance from the House of Wessex, forcing Æthelred's sons, who might have had claims to the throne, into exile to the court of their mother's family in Normandy. The same year, Cnut married Æthelred's widow, Emma, in a bid to further strengthen his image as a legitimate king. The marriage was likely negotiated by Emma in exchange for her sons' safety and an important position for her in Cnut's court, something to which the king appears to have agreed.

A year later, in 1018, Cnut passed his own law code, endorsed by Archbishop Wulfstan of York and drawing heavily from Anglo-Saxon legal tradition. Overall, it appears that it was Cnut's intention to be seen as the continuation of Anglo-Saxon kingship—as another in the line of succession and not a usurper of the throne. Cultivating a good relationship with the archbishop affirms this, as does Cnut's conscious attempt to reconnect with the peaceful and stable times of the past—especially those under King Edgar. For a foreign ruler who had conquered the English throne and forced members of the royal family into exile, Cnut was nevertheless quite tolerant of local customs, traditions, and religious practices. He was an active benefactor of the Church, especially in the south, donating lavish gifts to Canterbury and Winchester.

Although he put many Scandinavians into positions of power as ealdormen and in lower administrative roles, the makeup of English administration had again become Anglo-Saxon-dominated by the end of his reign in the 1030s. The relatively short-lived Viking nobles installed by Cnut were initially granted many lands throughout England, but their influence was kept in check by a similarly powerful Anglo-Saxon class of elites, led by Earl (a title increasingly used at this time) Godwin of Wessex. Earl Godwin and other influential nobles, though a new class compared to the old aristocracy, gradually accrued more power in England. This was made possible by Cnut's frequent absences, which created a small power vacuum in the kingdom, even though he would often delegate regents to rule in his name. Throughout the 1020s, Cnut campaigned extensively in Norway and defeated rebellions that challenged his rule in Denmark, for example.

All in all, Cnut the Great was a compelling ruler of the North Sea Empire and one of the most successful kings of England from the House of Denmark. The kingdom would be plunged once again into a succession struggle upon his death in 1035. His son, Harold Harefoot, acted as king for the following five years, although he was not crowned until 1037 due to the nobility's hesitation to declare their support for him. His half-brother, Harthacnut, was supposed to inherit the throne but was absent, trying to consolidate his position in Denmark, much like his father. Only after the death of Harold Harefoot in 1040 did Harthacnut return to England to claim the throne peacefully.

Restoration of the House of Wessex

Harthacnut was the last member of the House of Denmark to rule England in the eleventh century, and his reign was very short-lived—the king suffered a stroke in early 1042 and died in June of that year. The question of succession was again up in the air, but the transition of power was smooth and unchallenged this time. Sometime before his death, Harthacnut, perhaps realizing his ailing age, had invited Edward, son of Æthelred the Unready and Emma of Normandy, back to England. It is likely that since Harthacnut was unmarried with no children, he saw Edward as a natural successor—a sentiment that was shared among the English public, including the elites. This is alluded to in the *Chronicle*, which mentions that the people of England had chosen Edward as the next king. However, he was also the only logical candidate to take over the throne after Harthacnut. So, the elites' support for him does not necessarily mean Edward was their preferred choice as king.

Edward's reign as King of England would last for about twenty-three years until January 1066, making him the longest-reigning monarch in England since his father, Æthelred. The early years of Edward as king were naturally marked by political intrigue. Despite his royal lineage, he was virtually unknown since he had spent most of his early years in exile in Normandy with his mother's family. In fact, Edward, already about forty years old when he ascended the throne, was a much more foreign ruler than Cnut, Harold Harefoot, or Harthacnut had been. Life in exile had made him a Norman French who spoke French in private. His royal court was also comprised of figures who had been close allies of Cnut, such as Earl Godwin of Wessex and Siward of Northumbria. Naturally, these actors had accrued much more influence in England than the new king, so the first few years of Edward's reign were spent in endless political maneuvering.

Edward was forced to accept the fact that he did not have the leverage to exercise authority over his more powerful subjects. He must cater to their needs and demands to gain favor among the English and Danish aristocracy of his kingdom. It was only after making concessions to these interest groups that Edward was finally crowned as king on Easter Day in 1043, about two years since his arrival in England when Harthacnut had still been alive.

Godwin of Wessex was the earl whose support Edward most desperately needed. An experienced earl of English origins, Godwin had been part of the royal court for many years and held considerable sway in the kingdom. To expand his power, Edward realized he had to give something to the earl of Wessex in return—and he did.

At first, he granted Godwin's sons, Sweyn and Harold, earldoms in the West Midlands and East Anglia, and then married Godwin's daughter Edith in January of 1045. This significantly increased the influence of Godwin and his family, but it was not long before the earl and King Edward became rivals, especially over foreign policy matters. Most importantly, Edward decided not to campaign in Denmark to help Danish King Sweyn Estridsson against the Norwegian King Magnus' invasion even though King Sweyn, supported by Godwin, had personally asked for Edward's help. Godwin wanted to help King Sweyn because King Magnus aspired to invade England and claim the throne for himself, something that never transpired because of Magnus' death in 1047.

Tensions between King Edward and Earl Godwin further escalated in 1051-1052 when Edward appointed his Norman friend Robert of Jumièges as the new Archbishop of Canterbury despite the English clergy and Godwin favoring another candidate. Robert had come to England with Edward in 1041 and had been the bishop of London since 1043. He was one of Edward's closest allies since the beginning, and his appointment as the new archbishop further reduced Godwin's influence in the kingdom. Edward also appointed Norman clergy and nobles to positions of power within his kingdom, a naturally unpopular move for the English aristocracy. To gain some favor with the public, Edward then proceeded to disband the royal fleet, viewing it as an unnecessary tax burden.

By then, however, the relationship between Edward and Godwin had been strained, and an incident involving Edward's brother-in-law Count Eustace of Boulogne put the kingdom on the brink of civil war. Eustace and his Norman men got into a fight with locals in Dover, and Edward demanded that Godwin, as the earl who presided over Kent, punish the townspeople. Godwin refused. Archbishop Robert, a close friend and ally of Edward, then accused Godwin of plotting a conspiracy against the king, prompting earls loyal to Edward—Siward and Leofric—to muster their men and prepare for a fight with Godwin. Godwin, on the other hand, was supported by his sons Harold and Sweyn, who also prepared to go to battle. Tensions were as high as ever, but in the end, neither side was ready to fight. As a result, Godwin and his sons fled. Harold went to

Ireland, while Godwin and Sweyn went to Flanders. Having successfully expelled his opponents, Edward, endorsed by Archbishop Robert, divorced his wife and sent her to a nunnery.

Sweyn Godwinson died in exile, but his father and brother recouped their losses and returned to England in 1052 with a large army to confront Edward. This time, support for the king was not as firm. Edward negotiated a settlement with Godwin and Harold, reinstating them to their old positions and agreeing to get rid of the Normans in his court. In fact, the domains of Godwin and Harold were expanded at the expense of those held by the king and his Norman allies, which was supported by earls Siward and Leofric, who kept their lands as part of the agreement. Edward also took Edith back as his wife. He had to accept that, after a crisis that spanned two years, the power of the Godwin family had only increased.

Throughout the 1050s, as all the old prominent members of the court, including Godwin, died, Edward decided to grant even more lands to members of his family. Harold Godwinson was appointed as the new Earl of Wessex, while his younger brothers Tostig, Gyrth, and Leofwine were promoted to dominant positions in Northumbria, East Anglia, and the southwestern Midlands. This placed considerable influence in the hands of the Godwinson family, who were now just as powerful as the king himself.

Though most of the Godwinsons' power was concentrated in southern England, control of these earldoms gave them the ability to collect taxes, raise armies, and preside over local political and judicial affairs. Contemporary sources give us limited insights into Edward's intentions. It is unknown whether he believed he had been forced to give up such control and influence. This is a logical explanation if we consider that Edward gradually withdrew from active political affairs in the second half of the 1050s, increasingly spending his time away hunting, for example. He devoted less attention to both domestic and foreign policy affairs. Harold and Tostig Godwinson campaigned against the Welsh and the Scots in this period, not the king. Thus, the House of Wessex under King Edward had once again declined about fifteen years after its restoration as the ruling family of England in 1042.

As Edward's power and influence gradually declined well into his reign, the obvious question of succession to the throne became more prominent. Edward had no children, and it was not exactly clear who he favored as the next king. The fact that Edward never named a successor caused the whole crisis in 1066 after his death.

William of Normandy was perhaps the most unlikely claimant to the throne. An illegitimate son of Duke Robert I of Normandy, he would take quite a while to consolidate his power in the duchy before he was in a position to throw in his bid for the throne of England. William was related to Edward—he was the king's cousin once removed—but this relationship was by no means enough to make him a logical candidate in the eyes of his rivals, especially Harold Godwinson.

Importantly, William claimed Edward had promised him the throne of England in secret during the crisis of 1051-1052. Few contemporary sources mention that such a meeting took place between Edward and William. For example, only in the D version of the *Anglo-Saxon Chronicle* is the event even mentioned. It states that William visited Edward in 1051, perhaps to support the English king in a time of crisis against Godwin and his family. At the time, however, William was involved in a war in the County of Anjou, so his visit with Edward is unlikely.

Even if William did visit Edward, it is unclear whether the king entrusted him with succession. Norman sources mention another meeting taking place between William and Archbishop Robert, who had supposedly traveled as a dignitary on Edward's behalf to bring the Norman duke the news that he had been chosen as successor. However, the sources do not provide many details about the nature of this visit.

Alongside William of Normandy, whose potential candidacy as the next king remained relatively unknown to the English until 1006, there was also a bid for King Edward's exiled nephew—Edward the Exile. He was the son of Edmund Ironside, who had been forced to flee England in 1016 after the conquest of Cnut. Edmund had returned to England in 1057 with his family but died soon afterward and was buried in London. Instead, it was his five-year-old son Edward Ætheling who was next in line in the House of Wessex. All other male members of the House of Wessex had died by then. However, Edward was too young, and his mother held too little influence to properly press his claim during King Edward's lifetime, let alone after his death. By the time of Edward Ætheling's arrival in court, King Edward had already become passive at attending to state affairs, having delegated most of the work to the Godwinsons. Young Edward was thus never involved in royal matters, and the fact that he had no army, unlike William, made his candidacy as the next king even weaker.

The Norman Conquest

The events of 1066—one of the most important dates in English history—are very complicated because of the intricate relationships between the different actors during the crisis that followed Edward's death. Edward died in early January and probably entrusted the kingdom to Harold Godwinson, the most obvious candidate for becoming the next king.

Harold was Edward's brother-in-law, the most powerful earl in the kingdom with vast domains. He came from a respected and well-established family, had experience in governance and warfare, and was largely supported by other earls. Importantly, Harold was also of Anglo-Saxon origin from a local family, giving him an advantage over William. And while Edgar Ætheling was from the royal House of Wessex, the elites could not have pledged their support solely based on this factor. Finally, as if all these factors had not been enough, Harold claimed that King Edward had made him the successor on his deathbed.

Still, Harold's hasty coronation on the same day Edward was buried shows his adamance to become king and his potential awareness that others were just as capable of asserting their power in England.

One such contender was King Harald Hardrada of Norway. Hardrada's involvement in the power struggle had partially been a matter of chance. An experienced warrior who had spent his youth as a military commander in the Kievan Rus and the Byzantine Empire, Hardrada had become the king of Norway in 1046. An ambitious individual, he wished to also claim the throne of Denmark but failed to achieve this despite launching many raids into the Danish territories. Though the throne of England had never been among King Harald's objectives, he was invited as a claimant in late 1065 by Tostig Godwinson, who had by then strained his relationship with his brother Harold.

To better understand the struggles of 1066, it is thus important to examine the events of 1065 that turned Tostig against Harold—more specifically, the rebellion in Northumbria against Tostig.

Tostig had served as Northumbria's earl for about a decade, but the locals were unhappy with his rule. While Tostig was in the south visiting King Edward, the Northumbrians revolted, taking control of York and sacking Tostig's estate there. Their main demand was the expulsion of

Earl Tostig and the installation of Morcar, the younger brother of Earl Edwin of Mercia, as the new earl. The rebels pushed as far south as the East Midlands, pillaging Tostig's lands and pressing their demands before a peace was negotiated by Harold Godwinson. Tostig was stripped of his earldom and forced into exile. He was furious, believing that Harold had incited the rebellion and used it to expand his own influence in the north at the expense of his brother.

Around the same time, Harold had also married the sister of Earl Eadwig and the newly appointed Earl Morcar, securing an alliance with this powerful English family. Harold likely intended to build as many good relationships with the locals as possible so they would support his candidacy as king after Edward's death.

Tostig, feeling betrayed by his brother and the future king, fled to Flanders, where he assembled a small force and tried to return to England, possibly intending to become king. His attempt was unsuccessful, however, as Harold's forces easily repelled Tostig's fleet, forcing him to flee to the court of King Malcolm of Scotland.

In Scotland, Tostig Godwinson joined King Harald Hardrada of Norway, who had already launched his invasion to take the English throne. It is possible that Tostig invited Harald to throw in his bid for the throne, hoping to regain his earldom as a reward. For Hardrada, who envisioned himself as the next king of England and the reviver of Cnut the Great's North Sea Empire, Tostig could have proven a valuable ally in cementing his position as king.

Hardrada, who had assembled a sizeable army in the spring, landed in the Orkney Islands in early September, which were controlled by Norway. Then, he moved on to the town of Dunfermline on the southeastern coast of Scotland, where he met Tostig and King Malcolm of Scotland. Tostig, with his small force that paled in comparison to Hardrada's, joined the Norwegians and set sail for Northumbria.

While the Norwegians under Harald Hardrada were pillaging the Northumbrian countryside throughout September of 1066, the news of King Edward's death had already reached William of Normandy. The duke had already prepared a large fleet to cross the English Channel in late summer, but he was delayed by unfavorable weather. The exact size of William's army is unknown, and many sources greatly exaggerate the number of men at his disposal in 1066. It can be assumed that William had assembled a force of about 10,000 men, having mustered up his army from not only Normandy but also Brittany, where he had campaigned in previous years.

Luckily for William, King Harold Godwinson of England had already moved north to meet Harald Hardrada when he decided to cross the channel in late September. Throughout the summer, the English king had maintained a fleet that patrolled the southern shores of England, anticipating a potential invasion from William. Seeing that there was a more immediate threat in the northern part of his kingdom, Harold Godwinson marched to Northumbria to confront the Norwegians.

Covering a distance of about twenty-five miles per day, Harold and his army's march from London to York took only nine days—an exceptionally small amount of time. Still, when they arrived on September 25, they found the city decimated by Harald Hardrada. The Norwegian force had moved east and encamped at the village of Stamford Bridge. The English quickly proceeded to the village, trying to catch the Norwegians off-guard.

The ensuing battle resulted in heavy casualties on both sides. Chroniclers describe a vicious battle for the narrow crossing on the river, which was only defended by a single Norwegian. He stopped the initial English advance, killing tens of English soldiers before falling himself, having allowed the Norwegian forces to mobilize and form a defensive. Nevertheless, the English were victorious, and both Harald Hardrada and Tostig Godwinson were killed in battle. The survivors negotiated a truce with King Harold and agreed to sail back to Norway.

Stamford Bridge had been an amazing victory for the English. It was one of the most decisive victories over the Vikings in history, comparable to Æthelstan's triumph at Brunaburh more than a hundred years earlier. Certainly, it would have been instrumental in further legitimizing Harold's kingship, as he had successfully defended his kingdom from a large foreign invasion. Unfortunately for the English, however, William of Normandy's forces of landed at Pevensey just three days after the Battle of Stamford Bridge. The Normans proceeded to build a small fortification at Hastings, which they used as their headquarters while raiding the surrounding areas.

This called for a prompt response from Harold Godwinson, who was most likely already on his way back to London when he learned about William's invasion. He had left a part of his force in the north and decided to replenish his troops once he reached London, resting for a week. Then, he headed south to Hastings, where he met the Normans in battle. On October 14, at the Battle of Hastings, the English were defeated by the Normans. Harold Godwinson, the last crowned Anglo-Saxon king, was killed in battle, possibly after being struck by an arrow in his eye. His army was routed after the death of its leader.

The English fled to London, trying to organize further resistance and giving their support to Edgar Ætheling as the next king. Joined by earls Morcar and Edwin, they believed William would strike there next. However, William instead continued to ravage the southern countryside, moving east and eventually taking Canterbury. He successfully eluded the English forces that chased him down.

Eventually, the English leaders submitted to William one by one, and he was ultimately crowned King of England on Christmas Day, 1066, in the newly constructed Westminster Abbey. In exchange for submission, William spared the lives of the English nobles, including Edward. The era of Anglo-Saxon dominance in England was over.

Conclusion

It took William a lot of work to consolidate his power over England after the conquest of 1066. Many Anglo-Saxon nobles either tried to organize rebellions in the first few years of his reign or fled the kingdom. William, on the other hand, began replacing the English elite with Normans, though he kept the existing governmental and administrative systems in place. The Anglo-Saxon system was very sophisticated for its time, with England already divided into units that determined important matters, such as taxation. Instead of trying to shake up the system, William put some of the most prominent Normans in positions of power to better control the affairs of his kingdom.

He also promised amnesty to many of the old nobility, though he expected them to provide military support and raise armies from their domains in times of need. Many were stripped of their lands, which were redistributed to William's loyal followers, most of whom were either distinguished Norman commanders or noblemen themselves. Others chose to emigrate. The result of breaking up old estates and their redistribution is mentioned in the Domesday Book, a manuscript that recorded the results of the kingdom-wide survey of 1086.

In the Church, Anglo-Saxons were also increasingly replaced in favor of Norman clergymen. This ensured that the English Church would no longer persist as a potential rival of the Norman king.

In addition, William constructed several important fortifications throughout the kingdom, which he garrisoned with loyal troops to dissuade new rebellions from the English resistance. King William, nicknamed "the Conqueror," had to ensure that the situation in England was constantly under control as he was often absent, attending to matters in his home duchy on the other side of the channel.

All in all, after the initial changes implemented by William took root, a radically new England emerged. It had a new elite and was ruled by a new dynasty that had originated in northern France. The Norman Conquest also resulted in widespread social and cultural changes, such as the displacement of many Old English words and the increase of French influence. Latin was again used for official documents instead of Old English, a major change that affected the higher echelons of the new society.

It is estimated that fewer than 10,000 Normans settled in England during the post-conquest period by the beginning of the twelfth century, and they were well integrated into English society. In time, new distinctions emerged based on origins and dwelling place. Norman Englishmen, for example, were those born in England but of Norman origin. But these distinctions also faded with time.

In hindsight, William had achieved in England what no other conqueror could. He fundamentally transformed the nature of English society and never faced a real threat that could undo these changes. Similar processes had been attempted during the initial Viking conquest, but the scope of that invasion in the ninth century never reached as far as the Norman Conquest of the eleventh century. The Scandinavian invaders' motivations were very distinct from those of the Normans (who were themselves descendants of Vikings). William was accepted as the English king without much difficulty, and his descendants would continue to rule England.

Where does the Norman Conquest stand in the broader history of the Anglo-Saxons? It stands as the event that marked the end of Anglo-Saxon dominance in England, an era that had begun sometime during the fifth century. In fact, the consequences of William's conquest can arguably be best compared to the Anglo-Saxon settlement of Britain after the fall of Rome in the Early Middle Ages. The effects of both processes were widespread and long-lasting.

Still, the legacy of the Anglo-Saxons lived on in England to this day. The socio-cultural changes brought by the Normans eventually resulted in the development of Middle English by the fourteenth century as the mother tongue of most of England's population. It combined elements of Old English with new words brought by the Normans. What also survived was the political order established during the Anglo-Saxons' dominance. The post-conquest borders of England, as well as the country's modern borders, were largely forged in the Middle Ages by the Anglo-Saxons, as were many of the most important cities. The history of the Anglo-Saxons is compelling to examine, full of fascinating stories and memories that are still deeply rooted in popular culture.

If you enjoyed this book, a review on Amazon would be greatly appreciated because it would mean a lot to hear from you.

To leave a review:
1. Open your camera app.
2. Point your mobile device at the QR code.
3. The review page will appear in your web browser.

Thanks for your support!

Here's another book by Enthralling History that you might like

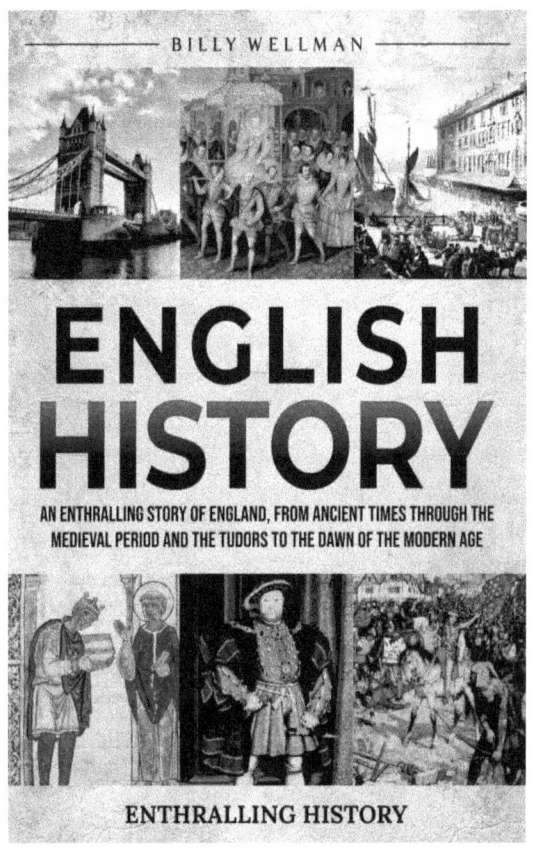

Free limited time bonus

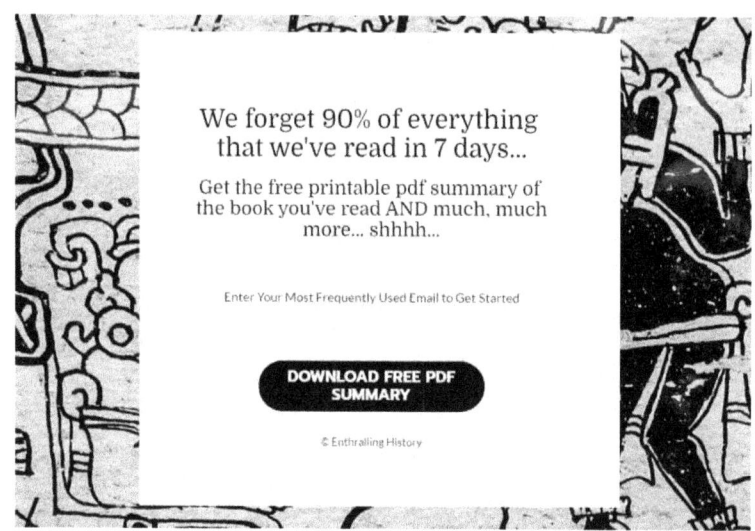

Stop for a moment. We have a free bonus set up for you. The problem is this: we forget 90% of everything that we read after 7 days. Crazy fact, right? Here's the solution: we've created a printable, 1-page pdf summary for this book that you're reading now. All you have to do to get your free pdf summary is to go to the following website: https://livetolearn.lpages.co/enthrallinghistory/

Or, Scan the QR code!

Once you do, it will be intuitive. Enjoy, and thank you!

Sources

Brown, M. P., & Farr, C. A. (Eds.). (2005). *Mercia: An Anglo-Saxon Kingdom in Europe*. Bloomsbury Publishing.

Brown, R. A. (1969). *The Normans and the Norman conquest / R. Allen Brown*. (1. publ.). Constable.

Chaney, W. A. (1960). "Paganism to Christianity in Anglo-Saxon England." *The Harvard Theological Review, 53*(3), 197–217. http://www.jstor.org/stable/1508400

Esposito, G. (2021). "The Viking Invasions of England." In *Armies of the Vikings, AD 793-1066*. Pen & Sword Books Limited.

Gebhardt, T. R. (2017). "From Bretwalda to Basileus: Imperial Concepts in Late Anglo-Saxon England?" In T. R. Gebhardt, C. Scholl, & J. Clauß (Eds.), *Transcultural Approaches to the Concept of Imperial Rule in the Middle Ages* (pp. 157–184). Peter Lang AG. http://www.jstor.org/stable/j.ctv6zdbwx.9

Higham, N. J., & Ryan, M. J. (2013). *The Anglo-Saxon world / Nicholas J. Higham and Martin J. Ryan*. Yale University Press. https://doi.org/10.12987/9780300195378

Hindley, G. (2013). *A brief history of the Anglo-Saxons*. Hachette UK.

Keynes, S. (1986). "A Tale of Two Kings: Alfred the Great and Æthelred the Unready." *Transactions of the Royal Historical Society, 36*, 195–217. https://doi.org/10.2307/3679065

Leyser, H. (2019). *A short history of the Anglo-Saxons / Henrietta Leyser*. (First edition.). I.B. Tauris and Company, Limited. https://doi.org/10.5040/9781350985148

Reynolds, S. (1985). "What Do We Mean by 'Anglo-Saxon' and 'Anglo-Saxons'?" *Journal of British Studies, 24*(4), 395–414. http://www.jstor.org/stable/175473

Williams, A. (2003). *Athelred the Unready: The Ill-Counselled King*. A&C Black.

www.ingramcontent.com/pod-product-compliance
Lightning Source LLC
Chambersburg PA
CBHW070334010526
44107CB00004B/507